A SEPARATE PEACE

John Knowles

SPARK PUBLISHING

Spark Publishing
A Division of Barnes & Noble
120 Fifth Avenue
New York, NY 10011
www.sparknotes.com

ISBN-13: 978-1-4114-0359-8
ISBN-10: 1-4114-0359-2

Please submit changes or report errors to www.sparknotes.com/errors.

Printed in the United States.

10 9 8 7 6 5

CONTENTS

CONTEXT

JOHN KNOWLES was born in 1926 in Fairmont, West Virginia. He left home at fifteen to attend Phillips Exeter Academy, an exclusive boarding school located in New Hampshire. After graduating from Exeter in 1945, he spent eight months as an Air Force cadet before enrolling at Yale University, from which he earned a bachelor's degree in 1949.

Over the next seven years, Knowles earned his living as a journalist and freelance writer, traveling in Europe and publishing a number of short stories. He befriended the noted playwright Thornton Wilder, a fellow Yale alumnus, who encouraged him in his vocation as a writer. In 1957, Knowles landed a job as an associate editor at *Holiday* magazine. Two years later, he published his first novel, *A Separate Peace,* to overwhelmingly favorable reviews; the commercial success of the book allowed him to devote himself to writing full-time. Since 1960, he has published eight other novels, including *Peace Breaks Out,* the companion volume to *A Separate Peace,* and a number of stories. None, however, has garnered the acclaim or audience that *A Separate Peace* has enjoyed and continues to enjoy today. Knowles has served as a writer-in-residence at Princeton University and at the University of North Carolina, and he continues to lecture widely.

The plot and setting of *A Separate Peace* were largely inspired by Knowles's experiences at Exeter. Like Gene Forrester, one of the novel's two principal characters, Knowles was a student from the South studying in New Hampshire during World War II—although he graduated a year too late to serve overseas during the war. Like his characters, Knowles also attended two summer sessions in 1943 and 1944, and even participated in a club whose members had to jump out of a tall tree into a river as an initiation stunt—a club much like the "Super Suicide Society of the Summer Session" founded by Gene and his friend Finny in *A Separate Peace.* He has told interviewers that he modeled the character of Finny after another member of this club named David Hackett, who later served under Robert F. Kennedy in the Department of Justice.

Yet while Knowles bases many of the book's circumstances on his own experiences at Exeter, he has always emphatically noted that the book's larger themes have no factual basis—that his own

CONTEXT

high school years were not plagued by the issues of envy, violence, and alienation that pervade the novel. He has written that he thoroughly enjoyed his time at the school and adds that he sought to convey his love and appreciation for it in *A Separate Peace*. Indeed, his treatment of "Devon" in the novel would seem to bear these statements out: despite its dark tone and perhaps pessimistic view of the human condition, the novel offers an ultimately positive and even nostalgic perspective of boarding-school life. Unlike other, more recent accounts of exclusive boarding-school culture, which have tended to portray the educational system itself as an oppressive force (in such films as *Dead Poets Society* and *Scent of a Woman*), Knowles chooses to locate his characters' difficulties not in the strict boarding-school system but within their own hearts.

Plot Overview

ENE FORRESTER is a quiet, intellectual student at the Devon School in New Hampshire. During the summer session of 1942, he becomes close friends with his daredevil roommate Finny, whose innate charisma consistently allows him to get away with mischief. Finny prods Gene into making a dangerous jump out of a tree into a river, and the two start a secret society based on this ritual. Gene gradually begins to envy Finny's astonishing athletic abilities, manifested in Finny's breaking a school swimming record on his first try. He thinks that Finny, in turn, envies his superior academic achievements, and he suspects that his friend has been taking steps to distract him from his studies. Gene's suspicions transform into resentful hatred, but he nevertheless carefully maintains an appearance of friendship.

Gene realizes that he has been grievously mistaken about the existence of any rivalry between them when, one day, Finny expresses a sincere desire to see Gene succeed. While still in a state of shock from the force of his realization, he accompanies Finny to the tree for their jumping ritual. When Finny reaches the edge of the branch, Gene's knees bend, shaking the branch and causing Finny to fall to the bank and shatter his leg. The tragedy is generally considered an accident, and no one thinks to blame Gene—especially not Finny. But when the doctor tells Gene that Finny's athletic days are over, Gene feels a piercing sense of guilt. He goes to see Finny and begins to admit his part in Finny's fall, but the doctor interrupts him, and Finny is sent home before Gene gets another chance to confess.

The summer session ends, and Gene goes home to the South for a brief vacation. On his way back to school, he stops by Finny's house and explains to his friend that he shook the branch on purpose. Finny refuses to listen to him, and Gene rescinds his confession and continues on to school. There, Gene attempts to avoid true athletic activity by becoming assistant manager of the crew team, but he feuds with the crew manager and quits. World War II is in full swing and the boys at Devon are all eager to enlist in the military. Brinker Hadley, a prominent class politician, suggests to Gene that they enlist together, and Gene agrees. That night, however, he finds Finny has returned to school. He consequently abandons his plans to enlist, as does Brinker. Finny expects Gene to take his place as the school's sports star now that he is injured. When Gene protests that sports no longer seem important in the midst of the war, Finny declares that the war is nothing but a conspiracy to keep young men from eclipsing the older authorities.

Finny tells Gene that he once had aspirations to go to the Olympics, and Gene agrees to train for the 1944 Olympics in his place. All the boys are surprised when a gentle, nature-loving boy named Leper Lepellier becomes the first one in their class to enlist. Gene and Finny go on training, shielded within their private vision of world events. During a winter carnival, which Finny has organized, a telegram arrives for Gene from Leper, saying that he has "escaped" and desperately needs Gene to come to his home in Vermont. Gene goes to Vermont and finds that Leper has gone slightly mad. Leper, who was present at Finny's accident, reveals that he knows the truth about what happened. Leper's ranting frightens Gene and makes him anxious about how he himself might react to military life. He runs away back to Devon. When Brinker hears of what has happened to Leper, he laments in front of Finny that Devon has already lost two of its potential soldiers—Leper and the crippled Finny. Gene, afraid that Finny will be hurt by this remark, tries to raise his spirits by getting him to discuss his conspiracy theory again, but Finny now denies the war only ironically.

Brinker, who has harbored suspicions that Gene might have been partly responsible for Finny's accident, wants to prove or disprove them definitively. He organizes an after-hours tribunal of schoolboys and has Gene and Finny summoned without warning. The boys on the makeshift tribunal question the two about the circumstances surrounding the fall. Finny's perceptions of the incident remain so blurred that he cannot speak conclusively on the matter; Gene maintains that he doesn't remember the details of it. The boys now bring in Leper, who was sighted earlier in the day skulking about the bushes, and Leper begins to implicate Gene. Finny declares that he does not care about the facts and rushes out of the room. Hurrying on the stairs, he falls and breaks his leg again.

Gene sneaks over to the school's infirmary that night to see Finny, who angrily sends him away. Gene wanders the campus until he falls asleep under the football stadium. The next morning, he goes to see Finny again, takes full blame for the tragedy, apologizes, and tries to explain that his action did not arise from hatred. Finny accepts these statements and the two are reconciled. Later, as the doctor is operating on Finny's leg, some marrow detaches from the bone and enters Finny's bloodstream, going directly to his heart and killing him. Gene receives the news with relative tranquility; he feels that he has become a part of Finny and will always be with him. The rest of the boys graduate and go off to enlist in relatively safe branches of the military. Gene reflects on the constant enmity that plagues the human heart—a curse from which he believes that only Finny was immune.

CHARACTER LIST

Gene Forrester The narrator and protagonist of the novel. When
    A Separate Peace begins, Gene is in his early thirties,
    visiting the Devon School for the first time in years.
    He is thoughtful and intelligent, with a competitive
    nature and a tendency to brood. He develops a love-
    hate relationship with his best friend, Finny, whom
    he alternately adores and envies. He often seems to
    want to lose hold of his own identity and live as a part
    of Finny, a tendency suggesting that he is strongly
    uncomfortable with his own personality. Yet the
    reader must infer this aspect of Gene, like much of his
    character, from the actions that he recounts rather than
    from any explicit statements regarding his mindset:
    Gene often proves a reticent and unreliable narrator
    when it comes to his own emotions.

Finny Gene's classmate and best friend. Finny is honest,
    handsome, self-confident, disarming, extremely
    likable, and the best athlete in the school; in short, he
    seems perfect in almost every way. He has a talent for
    engaging others with his spontaneity and sheer joy
    of living, and, while he frequently gets into trouble,
    he has the ability to talk his way out of almost any
    predicament. According to Gene, he is rare among
    human beings in that he never perceives anyone
    as an enemy, and never strives to defeat others.
    Finny's behaviors also suggest that he relishes pure
    achievement rather than competition. His fatal flaw
    is that he assumes that everyone is like him—that
    everyone shares his enthusiastic and good-natured
    spirit.

Leper Lepellier A classmate of Gene and Finny. Leper is a mild,
    gentle boy from Vermont who adores nature and
    engages in peaceful, outdoor-oriented hobbies, like
    cross-country skiing. He is not popular at Devon but
    seems to pay no attention to such things; only later

does the text hint at his desire to be closer to Gene and his jealousy of Finny's position as Gene's best friend. He is the first boy from Gene's class to enlist in the army, but military life proves too much for him, and he suffers hallucinations and a breakdown.

Brinker Hadley A charismatic class politician with an inclination for orderliness and organization. Brinker is very straight-laced and conservative. He has complete confidence in his own abilities and has a tendency to carry his ideas through with startling efficiency—at times even ruthlessness. Manifesting a mindset opposite to that of Finny, who delights in innocent anarchy, Brinker believes in justice and order and goes to great lengths to discover the truth when he feels that it is being hidden from him.

Cliff Quackenbush The manager of the crew team. Quackenbush briefly assumes a position of power over Gene when Gene volunteers to be assistant crew manager. The boys at Devon have never liked Quackenbush; thus, he frequently takes out his frustrations on anyone whom he considers his inferior.

Chet Douglass Gene's main rival for the position of class valedictorian. Chet is an excellent tennis and trumpet player and possesses a sincere love of learning.

Mr. Ludsbury The master in charge of Gene's dormitory. A stern disciplinarian, Mr. Ludsbury thrives on the unques- tioning obedience of schoolboys and works hard to restore order after the anarchic summer session.

Dr. Stanpole Devon's resident doctor. Dr. Stanpole operates on Finny after both of Finny's accidents. He is a caring man who laments the troubles that afflict the youth of Gene's generation.

Mr. Patch-Withers The substitute headmaster of Devon during the summer session. Mr. Patch-Withers runs the school with a lenient hand.

ANALYSIS OF MAJOR CHARACTERS

GENE FORRESTER

Gene is the novel's narrator, and he tells the story as a flashback, reflecting on his days at the Devon School from the vantage point of adulthood. He is the source of all of the reader's information in the novel and yet proves somewhat unreliable as a narrator—especially regarding insights into his own motivations. We first meet him as an older man returning to the place where he spent his adolescence; we thus initially attribute the wisdom of maturity to him and assume that he brings a certain degree of perspective to his memories of Devon. But even the adult Gene seems filled with fears and insecurities; his great worry, we realize, is that nothing has changed since adolescence—not the school buildings and not, most important, himself. We are then plunged into his memories of an idyllic summer session preceding his senior year in high school and his friendship with the athletic, spirited Finny. But what Gene initially presents as a perfect friendship soon emerges as nothing of the sort; his account of certain actions, along with statements that seem insincere or strained, soon betray his true feelings. Thus, Gene initially asserts that Finny resents *him* for his academic success. The reader quickly comes to realize, however, that it is Gene, in fact, who resents Finny—indeed, he resents Finny all the more for Finny's lack of resentment toward him.

Finny's fall constitutes the climax of the story, and, afterward, all of Gene's resentments fade away. By crippling Finny, he brings him down to his own level. As Gene and Finny subsequently become increasingly codependent, the reader comes to see that Gene's forced equalization of the two boys may have been darkly deliberate—it may have stemmed from a deep desire within Gene to blur his own identity, to lose himself in another. Gene's act of putting on Finny's clothes and standing in front of the mirror, feeling strangely peaceful, symbolizes his desire to leave behind his own self and become Finny. As the object of Gene's jealousy, Finny is, in the language of the novel's dominating metaphor, the object of Gene's own private "war"; yet, as the mirror scene and other episodes make clear, Finny is also Gene's great love. Because of Gene's own insecurities and smallness of self, however, he can realize this love only after crippling Finny, for only then can his mixed awe and resentment give way to pure devotion. It is never clear whether, in jouncing Finny from the tree, the young Gene is motivated by an unconscious impulse or a conscious design. What he certainly does not know, however, is that the fall from the tree will set in motion the chain of events leading to Finny's death, making Gene Finny's killer, the destroyer of the thing that he loves most. Gene's fatal tendency to blur love and hate, his deep desire to blur his own identity into Finny's, is at the core of the novel's tragedy.

FINNY

Although we see all of the characters through Gene's eyes, his perception of others is most significant in the case of Finny. Even as Gene resents his best friend and harbors dark, unspoken feelings of hatred toward him, he regards Finny at times with something akin to worship. His depiction of Finny contains a strong note of physical, if not erotic attraction. Finny is presented in classical terms, as a kind of Greek hero-athlete, always excelling in physical activities and always spirited—*thymos,* to use the Greek term. (These Greek heroes were, like Finny, fated to die young; the archetype was Achilles, who considered it preferable to live briefly and gloriously than to die of old age.) Energetic and vibrant, Finny is a tremendous athlete; friendly and verbally adroit, he is able to talk his way out of any situation. Finny finds himself in his element during Devon's summer session; the substitute headmaster enforces few rules and Finny can let loose his spontaneity and boisterousness without restraint. Yet while he constantly tests the limits and asserts his own will, he seeks neither to emerge "victorious" in any argument or contest nor to "defeat" competing systems of rule. Blitzball, the game that he invents in which everyone competes furiously but no one wins, perfectly embodies Finny's attitude toward life.

Finny's perspective on competition speaks to a more profound wisdom and goodness regarding other human beings. Just as he dislikes games with winners and losers, so in life he always thinks the best of people, counts no one as his enemy, and assumes that the world is a fundamentally friendly place. These qualities, according to Gene, make Finny unique; Gene believes that humans are fearful and create enemies where none exist. But Finny's inability to see others as hostile is his weakness as well as his strength; he refuses to attribute dark motives to Gene and he continues to subject himself to what may be a perilously—or even fatally—codependent relationship, never imagining that Gene's feelings for him are not as pure as his for Gene.

Moreover, by assuming that everyone thinks like he does, Finny often acts selfishly, insisting that he and Gene do whatever he fancies. This carefree, self-absorbed attitude is one of the roots of Gene's resentment toward Finny, though Finny, aware only of himself and seeing only the good in others, never seems to pick up on Gene's inner turmoil. Finny is a powerful, charismatic figure—perhaps too good a person, as he inspires in Gene not only loyalty but also jealousy.

Elwin "Leper" Lepellier

A quiet, peaceful, nature-loving boy, Leper shocks his classmates by becoming the first boy at Devon to enlist in the army; he shocks them again by deserting soon after. Both of Leper's decisions demonstrate important properties of the war: to the students at Devon, it constitutes a great unknown, overshadowing their high school years and rendering their actions mere preparations for a dark future. Leper's decision to enlist stems from his inability to bear the prolonged waiting period, his desire simply to initiate what he knows to be inevitable. Later, his desertion of the army again demonstrates a horrible truth: despite their years of expectation, the boys can never really be ready to face the atrocities of war.

Leper's descriptions of his wartime hallucinations constitute one of the novel's darkest moments. He proceeds to outline to Gene, with terrifying detail, the hallucinations that he suffered in the army, disproving Gene's belief that he, Leper, cannot possibly descend into bitterness or angry flashbacks when walking through his beloved, beautiful outdoors. This tension emphasizes the contrast between the loveliness of the natural world and the hideousness of the characters' inner lives. Most of Leper's visions involve transformations of some kind, such as men turning into women and the arms of chairs turning into human arms. In a sense, then, Leper's hallucinations reflect the fears and angst of adolescence, in which the transformation of boys into men—and, in wartime, of boys into soldiers—causes anxiety and inner turmoil.

BRINKER HADLEY

Brinker Hadley is, in many ways, a foil (a character whose actions or emotions contrast with, and thereby highlight, those of another character) to Finny. Also charismatic and a leader of the Devon boys, Brinker wields a power comparable but opposite to Finny's. Whereas Finny is spontaneous, mischievous, and vibrant, Brinker is stolid and conservative, a guardian of law and order. Finny, with his anarchic spirit and innocence, comes to be associated symbolically with the summer session at Devon, with its permissive atmosphere and warm, Edenic weather. Brinker, on the other hand, with his devotion to rules and his suspicious mind, is conceptually connected to the winter session, when the usual headmaster returns to restore discipline, the severe weather puts a damper on the boys' play, and the distant war intensifies, looming ever blacker on the students' horizons.

In many ways, Brinker represents the positive sense of responsibility that comes with adulthood. When he convinces Gene to enlist in the army, Gene moves toward accepting obligations and leaving the carefree realm of childhood behind. Yet Brinker also embodies the cynicism and jadedness of adolescence. He suspects the worst of Gene in contemplating his involvement in Finny's fall. Only at the end of the novel does Brinker fully come into maturity: his earlier support of the war is, in many ways, as naïve as Finny's insistence that the war is a big conspiracy; now however, he begins to resent the war for its injustice and madness.

Themes, Motifs & Symbols

Themes

Themes are the fundamental and often universal ideas explored in a literary work.

The Threat of Codependency to Identity

The central relationship in the novel—that between Finny and Gene—involves a complex dynamic of seeking to establish, yet being uncomfortable with, identity. Early in the book, the boys' relationship seems fueled, in part, by Gene's envy and resentment of his friend's dominating spirit. As Finny demonstrates his physical prowess, Gene feels the need to accentuate *his* academic prowess. Finny's fall from the tree, however, apparently purges Gene of his darker feelings and steers their relationship in a different direction so that codependency rather than envy characterizes it. The scene immediately following the fall symbolizes this evolution, as Gene dresses in Finny's clothes and sees himself as looking exactly like him. From this point on, he and Finny come to depend on each other for psychological support. Gene plays sports because Finny cannot, allowing Finny to train him to be the athlete that Finny himself cannot be. This training seems an avenue for Finny simply to live vicariously through Gene. But Gene actively welcomes this attempt by Finny, for just as Finny derives inner strength from fulfilling his dreams through Gene, so, too, does Gene find happiness in losing his own self (which he seems to dislike) in Finny's self (which he likes very much).

Thus, the boys' relationship becomes a model of codependency, with each feeding off of, and becoming fulfilled by, the other. This codependency preempts the development of their individual identities, perhaps dangerously: by living within their own private illusion that World War II is a mere conspiracy and continuing to believe that Gene (and Finny through him) will go to the Olympics and that the outside world can never curtail their dreams, the boys are refusing to grow up and develop their own ambitions and responsibilities. Not even Finny's death, though it separates them physically, can truly untangle Gene's identity from Finny's—he feels as though Finny's funeral is his own. In a sense, the reader realizes, the funeral is indeed Gene's own; so much of him is merged with Finny that it is difficult to imagine one boy continuing to exist without the other. It is perhaps only his ultimate understanding that Finny alone had no enemy that allows the older Gene to reestablish a separate identity—one that he considers, however, inferior to Finny's.

THE CREATION OF INNER ENEMIES

A Separate Peace takes place during wartime and is emphatically a novel about war—and yet not a single shot is fired in the course of the story, no one dies in battle, and only the unfortunate Leper even joins the military before graduation. Instead, Knowles focuses on the war within the human heart, a war that is affected by the events of World War II but exists independently of any real armed conflict. For Knowles—or at least for his narrator, Gene—every human being goes to war at a certain point in life, when he or she realizes that the world is a fundamentally hostile place and that there exists in it some enemy who must be destroyed. The novel implicitly associates this realization of the necessity of a personal war with adulthood and the loss of childhood innocence. For most of Gene's classmates, World War II provides the catalyst for this loss, and each reacts to it in his own way—Brinker by nurturing a stance of bravado, for example, and Leper by descending into madness.

Gene himself, though, states that he fought his own war while at Devon and killed his enemy there. The obvious implication is that Finny, as the embodiment of a spirit greater than Gene's own, was his enemy, casting an unwavering shadow over Gene's life. One might alternatively interpret Gene's statement to mean that this enemy was himself, his own resentful, envious nature, which he "killed" either by knocking Finny from the tree or by obtaining forgiveness from Finny for doing so. In either case, the overall theme is clear: all humans create enemies for themselves and go to war against them. Everyone, that is, except Finny, the champion of innocence, who refuses to believe that anyone could be his enemy. In a sense, Finny's death is inevitable: his innocence makes him too good for the war-torn and inimical world in which the rest of humanity lives.

MOTIFS

Motifs are recurring structures, contrasts, and literary devices that can help to develop and inform the text's major themes.

TRANSFORMATIONS

There are a number of significant transformations within the course of *A Separate Peace*. Finny is transformed from a healthy athlete into a cripple after his accident and then sets about transforming Gene into an athlete in his stead. These developments function as part of the broader process by which Gene's identity blurs into Finny's, a transformation symbolized by Gene's putting on Finny's clothes one evening soon after the accident. Meanwhile, the summer session at Devon, a time of peace and carefree innocence, metamorphoses into the winter session, in which rules and order hold sway and the darkness of the war encroaches on Devon. In a broad sense, the novel is intimately concerned with the growth of boys into men. The horrifying visions of transformation that drive Leper from the army—men turning into women, men's heads on women's bodies—embody all of the anxieties that plague his classmates as they deal with the joint, inevitable onset of war and adulthood.

ATHLETICS

A Separate Peace is filled with athletic activities, from the tree-climbing that is central to the plot to swimming, skiing, and snowball fights. For the most part, these games shed light on the character of Finny, who is a tremendous athlete but who nevertheless despises competition (in contrast to Gene) and imagines athletics as a realm of pure vitality and achievement, without winners and losers. This mindset is evident in the way that he behaves after breaking the school swimming record—he refuses to let Gene tell anyone about his feat—and in the game of blitzball, which he invents. Blitzball is the perfect game for Finny because it requires tremendous exertion and agility yet is impossible to win and focuses on pure athleticism rather than the defeat of opponents.

SYMBOLS

Symbols are objects, characters, figures, and colors used to represent abstract ideas or concepts.

THE SUMMER AND WINTER SESSIONS AT DEVON

The summer session at Devon is a time of anarchy and freedom, when the teachers are lenient and Finny's enthusiasm and clever tongue enable him to get away with anything. This session symbolizes innocence and youth and comes to an end with Finny's actual and symbolic fall, which ushers in the winter session, a time embodied by the hardworking, order-loving Brinker Hadley. The winter session is dark, disciplined, and filled with difficult work; it symbolizes the encroaching burdens of adulthood and wartime, the latter of which intrudes increasingly on the Devon campus. Together, then, the two sessions represent the shift from carefree youth to somber maturity. Finny, unwilling or perhaps unable to face adulthood, dies and thus never enters into this second, disillusioning mode of existence.

FINNY'S FALL

Finny's fall, the climax of the novel, is highly symbolic, as it brings to an end the summer session—the period of carefree innocence—and ushers in the darker winter session, filled with the forebodings of war. So, too, does Finny's fall demonstrate to Gene that his resentment and envy are not without consequences, as they lead to intense feelings of shame and guilt. The literal fall, then, symbolizes a figurative fall from innocence—like Adam and Eve, who eat from the Tree of Knowledge and are consequently exiled from the Garden of Eden into sin and suffering, the students at Devon, often represented by Gene, are propelled from naïve childhood into a knowledge of good and evil that marks them as adults.

WORLD WAR II

World War II symbolizes many notions related to each other in the novel, from the arrival of adulthood to the triumph of the competitive spirit over innocent play. Most important, it symbolizes conflict and enmity, which the novel—or at least the narrator, Gene—sees as a fundamental aspect of adult human life. All people eventually find a private war and private enemy, the novel suggests, even in peacetime, and they spend their lives defending themselves against this enemy. Only Finny is immune to this spirit of enmity, which is why he denies that the war exists for so long—and why, in the end, Gene tells him that he would be no good as a soldier—because he doesn't understand the concept of an enemy. It is significant that the war begins to encroach upon the lives of the students with any severity only after Finny's crippling fall: the spirit of war can hold unchallenged influence over the school only after Finny's death.

Summary & Analysis

Chapter 1

Summary

Gene Forrester, the narrator of the story, returns to the Devon School in New Hampshire, fifteen years after being a student there. He walks around the campus and notices that everything seems well preserved, as if a coat of varnish had been applied to the buildings, keeping them just as they were during his time there. He reflects on how fearful he was in those days—the early 1940s, while World War II raged in Europe—and decides to visit the two places that he most closely associates with that fear. The first is a marble staircase in one of the academic buildings, which Gene decides must be made of incredibly hard stone, since the depressions created by students' feet over the years are still shallow. After staring at these steps for a time, he goes back outside, passing the dormitories and the gymnasium, ruining his shoes as he trudges across the soggy playing fields in the rain. He eventually reaches the river and searches for a specific tree on its banks, which he locates with some difficulty in a grove of trees similar to each other. He identifies his tree by a number of scars on its trunk and by the way that one of its branches sticks out over the river. He reflects that this tree now seems so much smaller than it did during his youth, and a French proverb comes to his mind: *plus c'est la même chose, plus ça change,* meaning "the more things remain the same, the more they change." He turns to go inside out of the rain.

At this point, the narrative flashes back to the summer of 1942, when Gene is sixteen and standing at the foot of the same tree, which looms hugely like a "steely black steeple." Gene is there with his roommate Phineas, or Finny, and three other boys: Elwin "Leper" Lepellier, Chet Douglass, and Bobby Zane. Finny tries to persuade them to jump off a branch of the tree into the river—a feat that no student of their age has ever tried before. The jump is done by the older boys in the school as part of their physical training prior to their graduation and departure for the war.

Finny jumps first to show the others that it is possible, popping up out of the river to declare how fun the jump is. He then sends

Gene up the tree for his turn. Gene finds himself in a mild state of shock once he reaches the limb. As he ponders the plunge, Finny orders him to jump. Gene does so, but the other three boys refuse. The group heads back to the center of campus, Finny and Gene walking side by side. Finny tells Gene that he performed admirably once he had been "shamed" into jumping; outwardly, Gene denies being shamed into it, though he knows Finny's claim is true. The school bell rings, signaling dinner, and Finny trips Gene and wrestles him to the ground. After they get up, Gene walks faster, and Finny teases him for wanting to be on time for dinner. Gene tackles him, and they wrestle each other in the twilight while the others run ahead. Realizing now that their wrestling has indeed made them quite late for dinner, Finny and Gene skip the meal and go straight to their room to do homework.

ANALYSIS

This first chapter establishes the narrator's position as an adult looking back on an incident in his adolescence from a perspective of (theoretically) greater maturity and wisdom. Gene's wandering around the Devon campus in the opening scene creates a mood of dread that infuses the entire novel: the older Gene refuses to offer us any details of the story to come, but he makes ambiguous references to "specters" that haunted him as a young man, to "fear's echo," and to a "death by violence." These hints of darkness are explicitly linked to two places that the older Gene visits: the stairs and the tree, thus foreshadowing the revelation of the tragic events that take place in those two locations.

Although Gene has deliberately returned to Devon, in many ways his purpose seems to be to prove the impossibility of true return: he wants things to be different on this visit to his old school; he wants to have a sense that time has passed—and erased, we assume—the dark events of his high school years. Thus, he feels disconcerted at how new and varnished the school looks, as if it had been frozen in time since the days when he attended. The hardness of the marble steps he finds equally disquieting, for it makes them look "the same as ever." The most threatening aspect of these observations for Gene is what they imply about himself: that the passage of time hasn't changed him either. Indeed, he notes, the only things that have changed for him in the years since high school are the superficial matters of "money and success and 'security.'" When Gene discovers, then, that the tree by the river seems smaller than it did in his youth, he conveys a profound sense of relief. In citing the French proverb, however, Gene reverses the order of the clauses, which, when correctly ordered, translate to "the more things change, the more they stay the same" as opposed to his version, "the more things stay the same, the more they change." His emphasis, whether conscious or unconscious, on the idea of things staying the same suggests a fear that he has not changed. As the novel progresses, the reader gradually comes to realize what it would mean to Gene if he had not moved beyond the person he was during his high school years.

The flashback that begins midway through this first chapter and lasts throughout the entire novel creates an odd effect: once the narrative drops us back into the 1940s, the story seems to be told from the perspective of the younger Gene; yet the narrator frequently inserts commentary and philosophical musings that seem to come from the older Gene. This shifting perspective is part of a larger complexity in *A Separate Peace*: namely, the problem of the unreliable narrator. While we can assume that Gene recounts external events relatively accurately, he seems less forthcoming about his own emotions and desires. The reader is forced to read between the lines in many of the book's passages, especially those detailing Gene's relationship with Finny.

Gene presents his relationship with Finny as one of simple friendship, but subtle hints in the text signal the presence of darker currents below the surface. Indeed, the discrepancy between appearance and reality here does not arise only in Gene's account of events but persists within the story itself. Thus, not only does the narrator Gene declare himself and Finny to be on heartily good terms, attempting to give the reader a happy impression, but also the character Gene works to keep up this appearance to the other boys at the school.

However, the dynamics between the roommates are far from simple. First, power in the relationship is clearly skewed toward Finny, who easily makes Gene do things that he doesn't want to—like leaping from the tree branch and being involved in a wrestling match that makes them miss dinner. More important, it is evident that Gene resents Finny, although he doesn't explicitly admit it. Instead, he portrays Finny's perceived superiorities as mere annoyances: he says that he finds it "galling" that Finny weighs ten pounds more than he does. But the frequency of his allusions to Finny's handsome physique and grace (his harmonious movement, ability to "flow" rather than walk, perfect coordination) indicate that Gene possesses a much deeper envy. Although he later denies that Finny "shamed" him into jumping, he thinks to himself at the time, "Why did I let Finny talk me into stupid things like this?"

However, the description of Gene and Finny's high-school world suggests a much lighter mood than that of the scene that opens the novel. Gene's subtle resentment of his friend does not yet take on sinister overtones; at this point, the reader can easily dismiss it as a typical expression of natural adolescent competitiveness. The description of the sunny and carefree atmosphere at Devon during the summer session creates the sense of an idyllic life among the fields and trees; only later in the novel does the text establish a contrast between the beauty of nature and the darkness of the human heart. The only pressing sign of trouble at this point is the presence of the war. The text does, however, make a significant connection between war and the leap from the tree: the leap is normally undertaken by older boys, specifically as practice for jumps that they might have to make from torpedoed boats or troop vessels. Nevertheless, war in this passage is associated with boyish conceptions of bravery and adventure, not with brutality and hate.

Chapters 2–3

Summary: Chapter 2

Mr. Prud'homme, a substitute teacher for the summer session, comes by the next morning to discipline Gene and Finny for missing dinner, but he is soon won over by Finny's ebullient talkativeness and leaves without assigning a punishment. Finny decides to wear a bright pink shirt as an emblem of celebration of the first allied bombing of central Europe. Gene envies him slightly for being able to get away with wearing this color (which he says makes Finny look like a "fairy," or homosexual); indeed, Finny seems capable of getting away with virtually anything he wants to do.

Mr. Patch-Withers, the substitute headmaster, holds tea that afternoon. Most of the students and faculty converse awkwardly; Finny, on the other hand, proves a great conversationalist. As Mr. Patch-Withers enters into a discussion with Finny about the bombings in Europe, his wife notices that Finny is wearing the school tie as a belt. Gene waits tensely in expectation of Finny's reprobation, but Finny manages to talk his way out of the display of disrespect, accomplishing the impossible feat of making the stern Mr. Patch-

Withers laugh. For a moment, Finny's escape from trouble disappoints Gene, but he pushes the emotion aside, and the two boys leave the party together laughing. Finny suggests a jump from the tree and pushes Gene along toward the river. Finny declares that he refuses to believe that the Allies really bombed central Europe, and Gene concurs. They swim for a while in the river, and Finny asks if Gene is still afraid of the tree. Gene says that he is not, and they agree to form a new secret society—the "Super Suicide Society of the Summer Session." When they get out on the limb, Gene turns back to Finny to make a delaying remark and loses his balance. Finny catches him, and then they both jump. It occurs to Gene that Finny may have saved his life.

SUMMARY: CHAPTER 3

Thinking back on the near-disaster, Gene decides that while Finny may have saved his life, he wouldn't have been up in the tree in the first place if it weren't for Finny. He feels, therefore, that he owes Finny no real gratitude. That night, the Super Suicide Society gets off to a successful start as Finny convinces six other boys to sign on as inductees. Finny invents a list of rather arbitrary rules, including one that requires him and Gene to start each meeting by jumping out of the tree. Gene hates this rule and never loses his fear of the jump. Nonetheless, Gene attends every one of the nightly meetings and never contests the rule. Finny, who loves sports above all else, is disgusted with the summer session's athletic program, especially the inclusion of badminton, and spontaneously invents a new sport called "blitzball" one afternoon. The game utilizes a medicine ball that Finny has found lying around; competition in the game is not between two perpetually divided teams but rather shifts as the ball is passed from player to player. Whichever boy possesses the ball at a given moment becomes the target for the other players, who try to tackle him; the boy may try either to outrun the others or pass the ball off to another boy. The game produces no real "winner."

"Blitzball" gains immediate popularity, and Finny himself shows the most skill in it. One day, Finny and Gene are at the swimming pool alone, and Finny decides to challenge one of the school's swimming records. He breaks it on his first attempt, but only Gene witnesses it. Finny refuses to try again in public and forbids Gene to tell anyone about it. Finny remains uncharacteristically silent for a while before proposing that they go to the beach; the trip, which school rules strictly forbid, takes hours by bicycle. Gene agrees despite himself, and they slip away down a back road. The ocean is cold, the surf heavy, and the sand scorching hot. Finny enjoys himself immensely and tries to keep Gene entertained. They eat dinner at a hot dog stand, and each obtains a glass of beer by displaying forged draft cards. They then settle down to sleep among the dunes. Finny says he is glad that Gene came along and that they are best friends. Gene starts to say the same but holds back at the last moment.

ANALYSIS: CHAPTERS 2–3

Chapter 2 develops Gene's envy for Finny more fully. Watching Finny talk his way out of trouble, first with Mr. Prud'homme and then with Mr. Patch-Withers, Gene feels "unexpectedly excited" at the idea of his friend getting in trouble and then feels "a stab of disappointment" when Finny wriggles out. Gene tries to justify these emotions, reasoning that he did not want to see Finny punished for the sake of seeing him suffer but simply longed for the spectacle or excitement that the punishment would have brought. But this explanation seems false: when he says, "I just wanted to see some more excitement," Gene seems to struggle to convince even himself, adding, "that must have been it."

Moreover, Gene's excessive insistence that Finny is his best friend and that just being friends with someone like Finny is an honor seems forced. Although Finny clearly is a special person, what Gene doesn't say speaks as loudly as what he does: his last-second decision not to return Finny's profession of friendship on the beach betrays his envy. Thus, Gene is divided between admiration and resentment, love and hate—an inner conflict that, like the external conflict in Europe, grows more severe as the story progresses.

Gene's feelings about Finny point toward Finny's exceptional nature, and it is in these chapters that we begin to learn more about Finny as a person—though always, it is important to realize, through the perspective of Gene. Still, Finny's good qualities are obvious: the reader is quickly won over by his sense of fun, clever tongue, enthusiasm, and what seems to be genuine devotion to Gene. Apparent, too, is that he seems to have no need to prove his superiority over other people: he loves sports and physical activities, and he desires to be the best but has no desire to beat anyone else. His refusal to publicize his swimming feat seems to prove his modesty. "Blitzball," in which nobody wins but everyone competes, perfectly symbolizes Finny's attitude not only toward athletics but toward life in general.

Finny does have one fatal flaw, however, which becomes clearer later in the book: he exhibits an intense self-involvement and fails to perceive that others might be different from him, with different needs, desires, and fears. This egocentrism is evident in the way he assumes that because he wants to jump every night Gene will want to as well. Similarly, on the trip to the beach, Finny never even bothers to ask himself if Gene might prefer not to skip school to spend a night on the sand; Finny lets his own desires decide for both boys. It is important to note, however, that Gene never attempts to counter this aspect of Finny or to point it out to him: fearful of losing face with Finny, Gene never refuses him. Thus, the tensions latent in their friendship can never be brought out into the open; Finny never expects a "no" and Gene is never brave enough to give one.

The difficulty that Gene has in standing up for himself connects to the larger problem in the novel of Gene's sense of identity: throughout the book, Gene allows his own sense of self to be subsumed by Finny's stronger personality. Although this strange codependency is only hinted at in these early scenes, Gene's struggles to know and assert his own desires initiate a more general exploration in the novel of identity and what it means to be true to oneself.

Meanwhile, the backdrop to all these events is the summer session at Devon, a time when rules seem to be suspended. The summer session, like the war, serves as a large-scale metaphor for the lives of the characters. In practical terms, the session is characterized by a generally lax enforcement of school rules and a less-than-rigorous academic environment. But the resulting liberty that the boys enjoy—almost anarchic at times—represents a final stage of psychological innocence: the greenery and the boys' unrestricted romps evoke the paradise that preceded the fall of Adam and Eve into knowledge and sin. Like the biblical characters, the boys in *A Separate Peace* will also experience a fall, both figurative—a fall from innocence—and literal.

Gene and Finny's initial innocence seems to prevent them from consciously recognizing what may be homoerotic tensions in their relationship. Homosexuality is never mentioned explicitly by any character save when Gene says that Finny's pink shirt makes him look like a "fairy." But the relationships in the book are all between boys (we never see them interact with girlfriends or mothers, except for one brief scene with Leper's mother), and the central relationship contains hints of an almost sexual attraction between Gene and Finny. When the boys go to the beach, for instance, Gene remarks that his friend's skin "radiated a reddish copper glow of tan, his brown hair had been a little bleached by the sun, and I noticed that the tan made his eyes shine with a cool blue-green fire." Although the language is not expressly homoerotic, Gene's words suggest that the connection between him and Finny is, if not sexual, then at least strongly physical: the boys direct their affection toward each other's whole beings, increasing the intensity of their bond.

CHAPTER 4

I found a single sustaining thought. The thought was, You and Phineas are even already. You are even in enmity.

(See QUOTATIONS, *p. 53*)

SUMMARY

After he and Finny sleep on the beach, Gene awakens with the dawn. Finny wakes up soon after and goes for a quick swim before they head home. They arrive just in time for Gene's ten-o'clock test in trigonometry, which he flunks. It is the first time that he has ever failed a test, but Finny gives him little time to worry about it: they play blitzball all afternoon and have a meeting of the Super Suicide Society after dinner.

That night, Gene tries to catch up on his trigonometry and Finny tells him that he works too hard. Finny suspects him of trying to be class valedictorian, which Gene denies. Suddenly, however, he realizes that he does, in fact, want to be valedictorian so that he can match Finny and all of his athletic awards. Gene asks Finny how he would feel if he achieved the honor. Finny jokingly replies that he would kill himself out of envy; Gene feels that the jocular tone is a mere screen, however, and that there is some truth to Finny's words. Believing that the envy in their relationship is mutual, Gene now perceives a rivalry that he never recognized before. Highly disturbed, he concludes that all of Finny's overtures of friendship and insistence that Gene participate in all of his diversions are calculated to thwart him in his achievement of academic success comparable to Finny's athletic success.

Gene works to become an exceptional student and begins to surpass his only real rival, Chet Douglass. Finny cannot compete with Gene academically, but he nonetheless intensifies his own studying. Gene interprets Finny's hunkering down as merely an attempt to even out the sides of the rivalry, since Gene is an excellent student and a fairly good athlete, while Finny is an excellent athlete but a poor student. Despite Gene's suspicions of Finny, the two get along well in the weeks that follow.

The masters of the school, meanwhile, give up any pretense of discipline, and one day Gene tells Mr. Prud'homme about his trip to the beach with Finny. To his surprise, the teacher shows no concern about their rule-breaking. Gene continues to attend the nightly meetings of the Suicide Society so as to prevent Finny from suspecting that their friendship might be flagging.

One night, as Gene studies for a French exam, Finny comes into the room and announces that Leper Lepellier is planning to jump from the tree by the river that night and thus become a full member of their society. Gene doesn't believe that Leper would ever dare the feat and concludes that Finny must have talked him into the attempt in order to interrupt Gene's studying. Gene complains that his grade will suffer and begins to storm out to the tree when Finny tells him casually that he doesn't have to come along if he wants to study, as it is only a game. Finny says that he didn't realize that Gene ever had to study; he thought his academic prowess came naturally. He expresses admiration for Gene's intelligence and says that he is right to be so serious about something at which he excels. He tells Gene to stay and study, but Gene replies that he has studied enough and insists on going to see Leper jump.

As they walk toward the tree, Gene decides that there must never have been any rivalry between them after all. Moreover, he thinks that this latest interaction has proved that Finny is his moral superior: Finny seems incapable of being actively jealous of anyone. Finny proposes a double jump with Gene, and they strip and ascend the tree. Finny goes out onto the limb first, and when Gene steps out, his knees bend and he jostles the limb, causing Finny to lose his balance and fall with a sickening thud to the bank. Gene then moves out to the end of the limb and dives into the water, suddenly fearless.

> *Now I knew that there never was ... any rivalry ... I*
> *was not of the same quality as he.*
> *I couldn't stand this....*
>
> *(See* QUOTATIONS, *p. 54)*

ANALYSIS

Finny's plunge from the tree at the end of this chapter forms the climax of the novel. The events leading up to the fall show us Gene at his most petty and vicious. His resentment manifests itself as a sort of paranoia as he convinces himself that Finny is trying to sabotage his academic success. Ironically, Gene falls prey to the same flaw that afflicts Finny: just as Finny thinks that everyone shares his enthusiasms, so Gene assumes that everyone shares his jealousy and competitiveness. He is competing with Finny, so he assumes that Finny must be competing with him. Gene feels ashamed of the extent to which he is plagued by insecurity and envy; he overcomes this feeling of shame not by trying to improve himself but rather by convincing himself that Finny is just as bad as he himself is.

The dark, angry thoughts that Gene has about Finny contrast sharply with the idyllic, innocent spirit of the summer. The nature surrounding the boys, pure and wild, evokes an Edenic paradise (Gene himself calls the beach on which he and Finny sleep in Chapter 2 "as pure as the shores of Eden"). Gene's inner life soon shows itself to be the snake in this biblical garden. Gene is well aware of the tension between his mental state and his surroundings. In at least one scene, he actively goes to war with the beautiful weather: he describes how he wakes up on a perfect morning and forces himself to "guard against" the perfection of nature, for it saps his will to hate.

The need to maintain willful hate is one that Gene himself has invented: it is natural neither to this world nor, as Gene finally realizes, to Finny. (Indeed, it may not be natural to Gene, either, as he must force himself when in the face of beauty to persist in his resentment.) Unfortunately, the realization that hate is not intrinsic to Finny makes Gene even angrier than does his previous perception of Finny's enmity: if Finny does not, in fact, possess feelings of competitiveness and selfishness, this lack only makes him superior to Gene, who does possess them. Whereas Gene earlier envies Finny's athleticism, confidence, and ability to get away with things, he now envies Finny's goodness, which he finds too great to bear.

It is this later, deeper envy in Gene that stains all the events surrounding Finny's fall, raising the question of Gene's responsibility for the tragedy. Crucial to the novel's power, the facts of the event remain mysterious—to both the reader and the characters involved. We never know the extent to which the incident is deliberate; the jostling of the branch seems to arise more from Gene's hesitation than from any committed action. Nonetheless, the fall answers a deep wish in Gene, and there are times when Gene (and the reader as well) cannot help but assign a certain purposefulness—whether conscious or not—to the shaking of the branch. Ultimately, the degree of Gene's guilt in the incident is never resolved.

Regardless of the nature of the act, however, Gene's thoughts and behavior in this section create a problem of sympathy that persists throughout the novel. Gene is the narrator: he is the character with whom the reader most closely identifies. Despite his sympathetic qualities, Gene seems almost malicious at times—a corrupt, bitter figure who refuses to explain himself and so, despite our access to his consciousness, remains beyond our understanding and total commiseration. Whether or not we think Gene has deliberately caused Finny's fall, we begin to feel increasingly alienated from him. Thus, even as we become ever more invested in the story's outcome, we become distrustful of its narrator. This tension allows the reader to engage with the novel emotionally while still maintaining a critical stance and more freely analyzing the novel's themes.

CHAPTER 5

SUMMARY

Finny's leg has been shattered in the fall from the tree. Everyone talks to Gene about the injury in the following days but no one suspects him of any wrongdoing. No one is allowed to see Finny at the infirmary. Gene spends an increasing amount of time alone in his room, questioning himself. One day, he decides to put on Finny's shoes, pants, and pink shirt. When he looks in the mirror, he sees himself as Finny, and a wave of relief comes over him. The feeling of transformation lasts through the night but is gone in the morning, and Gene is confronted once more with what he has caused, whether or not deliberately, to happen to Finny.

That morning after chapel, Dr. Stanpole tells Gene that Finny is feeling better and could use a visit. He says that Finny's leg will recover enough for him to walk again but that he will no longer be able to play sports. Gene bursts into tears and the doctor tries to comfort him, saying that he must be strong for Finny. He notes that Finny asked to see Gene specifically, from which Gene concludes that Finny must want to accuse him to his face. Gene goes in to see Finny but, before expressing any of his own ideas about what happened, asks Finny what his memories of the incident are. Finny says that something made him lose his balance and that he looked over to Gene to see if he could reach him. Gene recoils violently and accuses Finny of wanting to drag him down with him. Finny explains calmly that he wanted merely to keep from falling. Gene then states that he tried to catch hold of Finny but that Finny fell away too fast. Finny tells him that he has the same shocked facial expression now that he did on the tree.

Gene asks if Finny recalls what made him lose his balance in the first place. Finny hints that he had a vague notion that Gene was the cause, but he refuses to accept this idea and apologizes for even considering it. Gene realizes that if the roles were reversed, Finny would tell him the truth about his possible involvement. He rises quickly and tells Finny that he has something terrible to say to him. Just then, however, Dr. Stanpole enters, and Gene is sent away. The next day, the doctor decides that Finny is not well enough to receive visitors; soon after, an ambulance takes Finny to his home outside Boston. The summer session ends, and Gene goes home to the South for a month's vacation.

In September, Gene starts for Devon by train and is delayed considerably. He catches a taxi at Boston's South Station, but instead of taking it to North Station for the last leg of the trip to Devon, he proceeds to Finny's house. He finds Finny propped up before a fireplace with hospital-type pillows. Finny is pleased to see him, though not surprised, and asks about his vacation. Gene recounts a story about a fire back home and then says that he was thinking a lot about Finny and the accident while at home. He now tells Finny that he deliberately shook the limb to make him fall. Finny refuses to believe him and grows furious. Gene realizes that he has injured Finny further with his confession and that he must take back his words, though he cannot do it now. Finny says that he will return to Devon by Thanksgiving.

ANALYSIS
It is significant that the first thing that Gene records himself doing after the tragedy is putting on Finny's clothes and mimicking Finny's

expressions in the mirror. This bizarre act symbolizes the extent to which Gene has blurred, and continues to blur, the line that separates his own identity from that of his best friend. To alleviate his guilt about his involvement in the fall, he seeks to escape his very self and find refuge in someone else's clothing, someone else's identity. Moreover, while becoming Finny allows Gene to escape his own guilty conscience, it also enables him to eradicate the feelings at the base of that guilt. Gene feels guilty about the accident because he knows how envious he was of Finny and cannot help but think that this envy somehow influenced his actions, even if only on a subconscious level. By dressing up as Finny, however, Gene purges himself of this envy by becoming the object of it.

It is again Gene's desire to be like Finny, or actually to be Finny, that sparks his confession: he admits what he thinks is his wrongdoing after realizing that Finny would have done the same were he in Gene's position. Ironically, Finny himself has no interest in Gene's declaration. In a sense, he is in denial; he has suspected a similar version of events—or so we assume from what he says to Gene about his "crazy idea" that Gene himself caused the fall—but he refuses to admit such a possibility. His life altered forever by the accident, Finny seems to need something to latch onto, and he latches onto his friendship with Gene. The relationship becomes the center of his life, especially once he returns to Devon in later chapters. Finny feels an increasing necessity to ignore the relationship's unpleasant aspects.

While Finny clings to the friendship, Gene makes an attempt to sever it. For while he may wish to mimic or even transform himself into Finny, he finds it too painful to maintain a connection to him as a separate person, to confront Finny and his injury from his guilty position. Structurally, Chapter 5 mirrors each of the two subsequent chapters, in which Gene formulates a plan that would cut his ties with his best friend, only to be thwarted by Finny or Finny's memory. Here, he wishes to confess to knocking Finny from the tree and thus destroy their friendship once and for all, but Finny refuses to accept the confession. In the next two chapters, Gene first attempts to give up athletics by managing the crew team and then plans to leave school and join the army. In each case, though, Finny—or thoughts of Finny—undercut Gene's plans. He appears not to realize Finny's influence; or perhaps, the novel suggests, he is glad that it is happening—glad, on some fundamental level that he cannot ultimately separate himself from his friend. All of Gene's attempts at severing the relationship fail and the friends sink into complete codependency, a process that begins in this chapter.

CHAPTERS 6–7

> *Listen, pal, if I can't play sports, you're going to play them for me . . .*
>
> *(See* QUOTATIONS, *p. 55)*

SUMMARY: CHAPTER 6

Gene sits at the first chapel service of the school year and observes that the school atmosphere seems back to normal, with all its usual austerity and discipline. He lives in the same room that he shared with Finny over the summer. The room across the hall, which belonged to Leper, now houses Brinker Hadley, a prominent personage on campus. After lunch, Gene starts to go across the hall but suddenly decides that he doesn't want to see Brinker. He realizes that he is late for an afternoon appointment at the Crew House. On his way, he stops on the footbridge at the junction of the upper Devon River and the lower Naguamsett River. He envisions Finny balancing himself on the prow of a canoe on the river, the way Finny used to do.

Gene has taken the thankless position of assistant senior crew manager and has to work for Cliff Quackenbush, an unhappy, bullying type. After practice is over, Quackenbush pesters Gene as to why he has taken the job: normally boys only tolerate the position of assistant in hopes of becoming manager the following year, but Gene is already a senior. Quackenbush begins to insult him, implying that Gene must be working as a manager because he cannot row; indeed, as Gene knows, disabled students usually fill such positions. Gene hits Quackenbush hard and they start to fight and fall into the river. Gene pulls himself out and Quackenbush tells him not to come back. As Gene walks home, he meets Mr. Ludsbury, the master in charge of his dormitory, who berates him for taking advantage of the summer substitute and engaging in illegal activities: in addition to his escape to the beach with Finny, Gene had participated in late-night games of poker and transgressed the rules in other ways. Gene only regrets not having taken fuller advantage of the summer laxity.

Mr. Ludsbury then mentions that Gene has received a long distance phone call. Gene enters the master's study and, calling the number written on the notepad there, soon hears Finny's voice.

Finny asks about their room and is relieved when Gene replies that he has no roommate. Finny says that he just wanted to be sure that Gene is no longer "crazy" like he was when he visited Finny and claimed that he jounced the limb. Finny then asks about sports and throws a fit when Gene tells him that he is trying to be assistant crew manager. Finny tells Gene that he has to play sports, for his sake, and Gene feels oddly joyful to think that he must be destined to become a part of Finny.

SUMMARY: CHAPTER 7

Brinker comes across the hall to see Gene and congratulates him on getting such a large room all to himself. He jokingly accuses Gene of having "done away with" Finny to get the room. Gene tries weakly to play along with the joke and then suggests that they go smoke cigarettes in the basement "Butt Room." Upon their arrival, however, Brinker pretends that the Butt Room is a dungeon and announces to the others there that he has brought a prisoner accused of killing his roommate. Gene tries to shake off the comment's hint of truth by making an overblown, obviously joking confession; he chokes, however, when he begins to describe jolting Finny out of the tree. Paralyzed, he challenges a younger boy to "reconstruct the crime," but the boy says simply that Gene must have pushed Finny off the branch. Gene ridicules the boy's conclusion, directing attention away from himself but eliciting the boy's hatred. He then declares that he must go study his French, leaving without having smoked.

To relieve wartime labor shortages, the boys shovel snow off the railroad and receive payment in return. On his way to the train station to go shovel, Gene finds Leper in the middle of a meadow, cross-country skiing. Leper says that he is looking for a beaver dam on the Devon River and invites Gene to come see it sometime if he finds it. Gene works on the same shoveling team as Brinker and Chet Douglass but finds the work dull and arduous. The boys shovel out the main line and cheer as a troop train, packed with young men in uniform, continues by them on its way. On the train home, the boys talk only of the war and their eagerness to be involved. Quackenbush says that he will finish school before going off to be a soldier, as he wants to take full advantage of Devon's physical hardening program. The other boys accuse him of being an enemy spy.

When they arrive back at Devon, the boys find Leper coming back from his expedition to the beaver dam. Brinker makes fun of him and, as they walk away, tells Gene that he is tired of school and wants to enlist tomorrow. Gene feels a thrill at the thought of leaving his old life to join the military. That night, after spending some time contemplating the stars, he decides to enlist as well. When he returns to his room, however, he finds Finny there.

ANALYSIS: CHAPTER 6–7

The shift in seasons from summer to winter parallels a more general shift in the novel's mood from the carefree innocence that preceded Finny's fall to a darker time in which a note of doom, associated with the coming war, grips the school. This shift is given a physical embodiment in the two rivers on campus. The fresh, clear, bubbling Devon River represents the summer session and its naïve carefree character. But this river flows into the salty, ugly, unpredictable Naguamsett, which is joined to the ocean and controlled by the large, global forces of the tides. This river can be seen as a symbol of a dawning era of bitter conflict and disempowerment for the boys. Whereas Finny, with his spontaneity and rebellious spirit, directs the activities of the former era, Brinker Hadley, a stolid, rigid personality and an advocate for authority and order, now succeeds him as the boys' leader. Indeed, not only does Brinker support order in the classroom and the dormitory, but he also functions as a force for order in the larger moral landscape. It is he who first suspects Gene's guilt and eventually insists on bringing out the truth and seeing justice done at whatever cost.

Gene's desire to manage crew seems to be an attempt to escape Finny's shadow, as it places him far from the central, physical aspect of the school's athletics program, in which Finny excelled. Yet the reader quickly realizes the irony of this attempt when Gene remarks that the job usually goes to disabled students: Gene, of course, is not disabled, but Finny is. Once again, it seems, Gene proves unable to separate his own identity from that of his friend. When the odious Quackenbush (a minor character whose absurd name suits his role as a much-disliked clod) makes fun of Gene for being "maimed," Gene responds violently even though he isn't maimed at all. One can argue that he is fighting for Finny—or, perhaps, that he is fighting as Finny. Gene himself is acutely aware of his increasing identification with his friend, especially when Finny insists that if he, Finny, cannot play sports, then Gene must play them for him. At this moment, Gene understands that he is losing himself and becoming a part of Finny. One might understand the joy that Gene consequently feels as stemming from a deep desire: he may dislike himself so much by now that his dearest wish is to abandon this self altogether.

In these chapters, the war takes on an increased significance in the novel, having lurked in the background thus far. As the title of *A Separate Peace* suggests, World War II plays a central role in the fabric of the story—yet it does so without ever directly affecting the lives of the characters. None of the boys goes into battle and none except for Leper even joins the army until after graduation. *A Separate Peace* is a war novel without tanks, guns, or bullets; it is the shadow of war and the knowledge of its approach that affects the characters. Gene, in his unwillingness to play sports, sees the violence of football as mirroring battlefield violence, and he imagines tennis balls turning into bullets. Indeed, his narrative betrays a sudden obsession with war and its images: he compares the snow to an advancing army and thinks of the flakes' slow accumulation as paralleling the almost undetectable yet steady encroachment of the war on the peacefulness of life at Devon.

Ultimately, the war has only an indirect and insidious effect on the students at Devon. It causes a tense feeling of unsettlement among the boys, disrupting their former lives yet never fully releasing them onto the new horizons at which it hints. The boys know that they will have to join the fighting eventually, but, still young students, all they can do is wait. They stand shoveling snow off train tracks while real soldiers ride on the trains to their assignments. The world is at war, but the Devon boys still exist amid a "separate" illusory peace. Only Leper, eccentric and gentle, seems untouched by the peculiarity of their situation and simply continues with his hobbies of skiing and nature-watching. Leper, in a way, is still in the summer session—still innocent, not yet fallen from grace. But the rest of the boys have moved on psychologically. Thus, Brinker's desire simply to enlist, to put a stop to the gray and fruitless waiting period, seems perfectly understandable, as does Gene's decision to join him. When Gene eventually abandons his plans to enlist, he does so based upon his relationship with Finny—not because he has ceased to hate the gloom of waiting or the feeling of uselessness.

CHAPTER 8

SUMMARY

Finny playfully criticizes Gene's clothes and grumbles about the lack of maid service. Gene responds that it is no great loss, considering the war, and he makes up Finny's bed for him. The next day, Brinker bursts in, about to ask if Gene is ready to enlist, when he sees Finny. He starts to make a joke about Gene's "plan"—to kill Finny and get the room for himself—but Gene cuts him off and explains to Finny about Brinker's suggestion to enlist. Finny's unenthusiastic reaction leads Gene to realize that Finny doesn't want him to leave. Gene now tells Brinker, to Finny's obvious relief, that he no longer wants to enlist. The roommates begin to make jokes, saying that they wouldn't enlist with Brinker if he were General MacArthur's son or even Madame Chiang Kai-shek of China. In the midst of these jokes, Finny tags Brinker with a nickname: "Yellow Peril" Hadley, referring to his supposed double-life as Madame Chiang Kai-shek.

As Gene and Finny make their way over patches of ice to their first class, Finny remarks that winter loves him; he knows this, he says, because he loves winter, and it must return his affection. He then suggests that they cut class to give Finny a chance to look at the school after his long absence. They set out immediately across campus for the gym. Gene worries that Finny is planning to stare at his trophies and brood, but instead they go down to the locker room and Finny asks Gene what team he has joined for the year. Gene tells him that he did not try out for any teams, attempting to defend himself by noting the diminished importance of sports during the war. Finny declares that there is no war, that it is all a conspiracy orchestrated by the adult establishment—by fat, rich, old men—to keep young people in their place. When Gene asks why the conspiracy has not been detected by anyone else, Finny replies that he alone can see it because of the extent of his suffering. His answer amazes both boys. An awkward silence follows, and Gene, wanting to break the tension, goes over to an exercise bar and begins doing chin-ups. Finny tells him to do thirty and encourages him with his tone of voice as he counts them aloud for Gene. Finny tells Gene that he wanted to be an Olympic athlete and that now he will have to train Gene to go in his place. Finny convinces Gene to undertake the training despite his objections that the war will preempt the Olympics in 1944. Finny begins to train Gene and Gene tutors Finny in his classes; they are both surprised by their progress.

One morning, as Gene runs a course around the headmaster's house under Finny's guidance, he suddenly finds his stride, running better than he ever has before. Mr. Ludsbury comes out to see what the boys are doing and Finny tells him that Gene is training for the Olympics. Ludsbury tells them to remember that all athletic training should be dedicated to preparation for war, but Finny flatly replies, "No." This response flusters Ludsbury, who mutters something and leaves. Finny muses that the headmaster seems to believe sincerely in the reality of the war; he concludes that Ludsbury must be too thin to be let in on the hoax run by the fat old men. Gene feels a flash of pity for Ludsbury's "fatal thinness," reflecting that he indeed seems to have always had a "gullible side."

ANALYSIS

By this point in the book, the reader recognizes the effect of Finny's fall on his relationship with Gene. Far from driving a wedge between them, the fall has instead resulted in a tightening of the strange bond between the two friends. "He need[s] me," Gene says to himself, watching his friend hobble into the shower, a realization sufficient to drive away his thoughts of joining the army. Were he to enlist, Gene would join Brinker Hadley in embracing adulthood and responsibility; in many ways, by staying by Finny's side, Gene inhibits his own development and process of self-discovery.

There are two possible explanations for how the fall can have brought the friends closer even though the events and emotions leading up to it seem to prove Gene undeserving of such a friendship. First, Finny does seem to harbor a genuine love for Gene, and, because he loves his friend, it doesn't occur to him that Gene might not love him back. As usual, he assumes that other people approach the world in the same way that he does. This attitude emerges clearly in his comments about winter: loving winter himself, he cannot conceive of the season harboring any enmity toward him, though Gene points out that winter is treacherous for someone on crutches. If one loves something enough, he insists, it must return that affection. One can argue that this assumption—that love is always reciprocated—is the foundation of his continued closeness with Gene.

But there may be a darker current underpinning the boys' closeness, working alongside Finny's innocent love for his best friend. We have already seen evidence of Gene's eagerness to lose himself in Finny, to give up his identity and live as a part of his friend. But now, in Finny's enthusiasm to train Gene for the 1944 Olympics, we observe how Finny, too, contributes to this process, welcoming this sacrifice on Gene's part. Denied the ability to live life to the fullest by his injury, Finny sets out to live through Gene by attempting to transform him into the athlete that he himself once was. When Gene achieves his breakthrough on the track and becomes a better runner,

Finny remarks that Gene has learned something new about himself through exercise. While this statement may be true, it also rings of cruel irony: perhaps all that Gene has learned about himself is how easily he can transform himself into a mirror of Finny.

Finny's coaching Gene more for his own sake than for his friend's would not be entirely out of character. As the novel makes clear, Finny has always been self-absorbed, and his injury only cements this aspect of him. This self-absorption manifests itself in his insistence that the war is a hoax created by fat, rich, old men. Finny's motivations in making this claim are all too apparent: everyone at Devon lives under the shadow of imminent military service, knowing that soon they will be called upon to go off to war—everyone except for the crippled Finny. His injury has placed him in a "separate peace," one that he doesn't consider a blessing; rather, he feels that it isolates and alienates him, excluding him from the common experiences of his classmates and the entire world. Finny cannot accept being left out: if the war cannot be a part of his life, then he cannot let it exist for anyone at all. When Mr. Ludsbury challenges this illusion by insisting that everyone must train for war, Finny's famous charm vanishes and he responds rudely. His curt contradiction of Ludsbury's statement constitutes one of the few moments in the book when Finny deliberately offends or acts coldly toward another person. His habitual friendliness, it seems, does not extend to those who challenge his self-preserving illusions.

The scene outside Mr. Ludsbury's residence is also important for the parallel that it sets up between athletics and war. Earlier, Gene compares various athletic events to battlefield combat, describing tennis balls as bullets and football players as foot soldiers. For Finny, however, the conceptual implications of these comparisons make no sense. In his world, athletics are ultimately anticompetitive and embody pure achievement, unconnected to either definitive victory or conclusive defeat. The rules that he devises for blitzball illustrate his notions about what sports are and should be: not one team pitted against another but sheer physical challenge, embarked on together. Knowles's novel suggests that Finny is singular in his attitude: as becomes apparent by the end, everyone else in the novel is a creature of war, living their lives in constant battle against whatever enemies they have engendered for themselves. These other characters extend their warrior mindsets to sports as well. Finny alone refuses to connect athletics and war because he doesn't understand the concept of an enemy.

CHAPTERS 9–10

SUMMARY: CHAPTER 9

Gene feels a profound inner peace as he trains with Finny, and he sometimes finds it hard to believe truly in the widespread confusion of the war. To everyone's surprise, Leper Lepellier, after watching a documentary about ski troops, enlists in January, which only makes the war seem even more unreal to Gene. Later, Brinker starts the running joke that Leper must be behind any Allied victory. Finny refuses to take part in these jokes, and as they come to dominate the conversation in the Butt Room, both he and Gene stop going there. He pulls Gene farther and farther away from his other friends until Gene spends all his time with him, training for the Olympics.

One day, Finny decides to stage a winter carnival and starts assigning tasks. Brinker organizes the transfer of equipment from the dormitory to a park on the river and has his mousy roommate, Brownie Perkins, guard several jugs of hard cider buried in the snow. The boys arrange a little ski jump, snow statues, and prizes, and Chet Douglass provides music on his trumpet. As the carnival begins, the other boys wrestle the cider away from Brinker at Finny's prompting and break into anarchic carousing. Everyone seems intoxicated with cider and life itself, especially Finny, who performs a wild yet graceful dance on the prize table with his good leg. Finny announces the beginning of the carnival's decathlon and has Gene demonstrate various feats of athleticism for the appreciative crowd. Amid the festivities, Brownie reappears from the dormitory with a telegram: Leper has written to Gene to say that he has "escaped" and that his safety depends on Gene coming at once to his "Christmas location."

> [I]f Leper was psycho . . . the army . . . had done it to him, and . . . all of us were on the brink of the army.
>
> (See QUOTATIONS, p. 56)

SUMMARY: CHAPTER 10

Gene immediately sets out for Leper's "Christmas location," meaning his home in Vermont. He takes a train and then a bus through the barren New England landscape and arrives in Leper's town early the next morning. He walks the rest of the way through the snow to Leper's house. All the while he refuses to admit to himself that Leper has deserted the army; he tries to convince himself that by "escape," Leper has meant an escape from spies.

Leper stands at the window, beckoning Gene as he approaches, and then bustles him into the dining room. Leper tells Gene that he has, in fact, deserted; he did so because the army was planning to give him a Section Eight discharge for insanity, which he says would have prevented him from ever finding work or leading a normal life. Gene makes a few uncertain comments and Leper suddenly breaks down, insulting him. He then accuses Gene of knocking Finny out of the tree. Gene kicks Leper's chair over. Leper's mother rushes into the room, declaring that her son is ill and demanding to know why Gene would attack a sick person. Leper then invites Gene to stay for lunch, which he does out of guilt. At his mother's suggestion, Leper goes for a walk with Gene after the meal. Leper suddenly begins sobbing and tells Gene of his odd hallucinations at training camp: officers' faces turned into women's faces, soldiers carrying detached limbs, and so on. Eventually, Gene cannot bear to listen to Leper any longer and runs away into the snowy fields.

ANALYSIS: CHAPTERS 9–10

Leper, who has been strictly a secondary character thus far, suddenly takes center stage in the novel, first by joining the army and then by deserting. Although Leper's classmates react with surprise, his decision is quite understandable. The war is the great unknown for the students at Devon, one that they will all have to face at some point. Leper, who is the oldest boy in the class, will have to enter it sooner than anyone else. The film about the ski troops gives him a chance to enter the war and the unknown through something he knows well—skiing. His proactive decision to enlist also offers him a sense of control and empowerment that would be absent if he waited to be drafted into the service.

Leper's decision affords the reader several insights into his classmates, as the boys react in telling ways. First, they respond with disbelief, and because they find the idea of Leper in the army so unimaginable, the war becomes to them more distant and alien than ever. Later, however, when they do begin to consider Leper's enlistment as a possibility, they turn the issue into a joke. Led by Brinker, they mockingly envision Leper as a war hero. Gene himself notes that by talking and laughing about Leper's heroics, he and his classmates are able to personalize the war. When they imagine one of their peers involved in grand historical events, the war suddenly seems more on their level, less intimidating; after all, if Leper can be a hero, then anyone can. Thus, the boys' anxieties about wartime failure, about being "the Sad Sack, the outcast or the coward," can be set aside.

That only Finny refuses to join in the joking is significant. He has no insecurities about being a coward or a poor soldier because he cannot be a soldier at all. Furthermore, to join in the make-believe about Leper's impending achievements would be to admit that the war is actually real—that it is not an invention of the fat old men, as Finny would have it. He prefers to remain instead in his separate world of sport, training Gene for the 1944 Olympics. The winter carnival that he organizes is part of this world; with its good-natured games, races, and meaningless prizes, it embodies the spirit of noncompetitive athletics that Finny cherishes. Indeed, it is at the carnival that we again witness Finny's spontaneous vibrancy. With the "winter carnival" he does not so much celebrate winter as transfer his earlier summer realm, in which his spirit of freedom and innocent jubilance dominates, into the colder season, interrupting and supplanting it. This supplanting is most evident when Brinker, who embodies the winter session and the rigid order that accompanies it, proves unable to stand up to Finny and his anarchic force. In a symbolic scene, Brinker tries to make the games proceed in an orderly fashion, only to be tackled by all of the other boys at Finny's command. At this moment, the spirit of whimsy and frolic overcomes the spirit of rules and duties; for now, if only for a day, Finny is the master of Devon, and Brinker must simply follow his lead.

The carnival is cut short, however, by the arrival of the telegram from Leper, just as the war, or news of the war, has interrupted the boys' youth and innocence. Leper has addressed the message to Gene and signed it "your best friend," which gives the reader pause: after all, Gene has only mentioned Leper occasionally. It is possible that Leper is simply deluding himself in closing his telegram this way and making a bid for Gene's sympathy. Nevertheless, the unexpected phrase serves to remind the reader that there are areas of Gene's life that he simply neglects or refuses to illuminate for us; his relationship with Leper may be one of them. With the words "your best friend," Leper also invokes Finny, who has seemingly come to monopolize Gene's affections in recent chapters. Indeed, when Leper writes these words, he may be thinking specifically of Finny and consciously trying to displace him. Perhaps Leper, de-siring Gene as his best friend, envies Finny and wants to disrupt their relationship. His anger toward Gene during Gene's visit and his unexpectedly violent verbal assaults can be explained, in part, by the obvious mental breakdown that he has suffered while in the army. But these outbursts also suggest a possibility that Gene never discusses—namely, that Leper feels excluded from Gene and Finny's friendship. This notion is further supported by Leper's later revelation of what he thinks happened on the tree the day that Finny fell.

Leper's account of his madness, which takes place against a backdrop of pristine Vermont snow, constitutes one of the book's darkest moments. Gene decides that Leper cannot possibly be "wild or bitter or psycho" when walking through the beautiful outdoors that he loves so much. Gene, however, is deluding himself—Leper soon launches into terrifying descriptions of the hallucinations that he suffered in the army. In light of Leper's torment, Gene's comment emphasizes the contrast between the loveliness of the natural world and the inner lives of the characters. Most of Leper's visions involve transformations of some kind, such as men turning into women and the arms of chairs turning into human arms. In a sense, then, Leper's hallucinations reflect the fears and angst of adolescence, in which the transformation of boys into men—and, in wartime, of boys into soldiers—causes anxiety and inner turmoil. Indeed, when Gene runs away from Leper declaring that the visions have "nothing to do with [him]" and that he "[doesn't] want to hear any more of it," he proves just how close to the bone Leper's visions have cut him: the nightmarish metamorphoses are a dark reflection not only of the transformations that he and his classmates face but also of Gene's own attempts to become Finny—to don Finny's clothes and lose himself in Finny's identity.

CHAPTER 11

SUMMARY
Gene returns to Devon from Leper's house and finds Finny in the midst of a snowball fight, which he has organized. Gene hesitates to join the fight but Finny draws him in. Gene asks Finny, who now uses a walking cast, if he is allowed to participate in such strenuous activities. Finny replies that he thinks he can feel his bones getting better. He adds that bones are often stronger in the places where they have once broken. Brinker comes to visit Gene and Finny in their room and asks about Leper. Gene tells him that Leper has changed dramatically and that he has deserted the army. Although

Gene's words are vague, Brinker immediately surmises that Leper has "cracked." He then laments having two people in his class already "sidelined," unable to contribute to the war. Gene realizes that this pair includes Finny and tries to gloss over the implication by saying that there is no war, hoping he can distract Finny by getting him to elaborate upon his conspiracy theory. Finny repeats Gene's denial but in an uncharacteristically ironic tone; his words seem to Gene to mark the end of his fantastical conception of reality—a perspective that included the possibility of the 1944 Olympic Games being held.

Time passes, and all of the eligible boys, except for Gene, take steps toward enlisting in some relatively safe branch of the military. One day, Brinker takes him aside and tells him that he knows that Gene has decided not to enlist because he pities Finny. He says that they should confront Finny about his injury casually, whenever possible, to make him accept it. He adds that it would be best if "everything about Finny's accident was cleared up and forgotten"—and that Gene might have a "personal stake" in such an outcome. Gene demands to know Brinker's meaning; Brinker responds tauntingly that he doesn't know but that Gene may.

Later that morning, Gene reads Finny part of a Latin translation (from Caesar's *Gallic Wars*) that he has done for him. Though Finny doesn't believe in Caesar, he does finally admit the existence of World War II. He says that he had to accept the reality of the war when Gene told him that it had caused Leper to go crazy. If something can make a person go crazy, Finny says, it must be real. He adds that he did not completely accept Gene's description of Leper at first but that it was confirmed when he saw Leper hiding in the bushes that morning after chapel. Gene is shocked to hear that Leper is back at Devon. They decide not to tell anyone and begin joking about Gene's amazing feats at the imaginary 1944 Olympics.

That night, Brinker comes into Gene and Finny's room with several other boys and takes Gene and Finny off to the Assembly Hall, where he has gathered an audience and a panel of judges for an inquiry into the cause of Finny's accident. Brinker asks Finny to explain in his own words what happened on the tree, and Finny reluctantly says that he lost his balance and fell. Boys from the makeshift tribunal ask what caused him to lose his balance in the first place and inquire about Gene's whereabouts at the time. Finny says that he thinks that Gene was at the bottom of the tree and Gene agrees that he was but that he cannot remember exactly what happened. But Finny then remembers that he had suggested a double jump and that they were climbing the tree together. Gene struggles to defend the discrepancy between their stories. Brinker laments that Leper is not there, as he could have remembered everyone's exact position.

Finny quietly announces that he saw Leper slip into Dr. Carhart's office that morning; the two boys are sent to find him. Gene tells himself that Leper is crazy and that even if his testimony implicates Gene, no one will ever accept it. After a while, the boys return with Leper, who seems strangely confident and composed. The tribunal asks him what happened and he replies that he saw two people on the tree silhouetted against the sun and saw one of them shake the other one off the branch. Brinker asks Leper to name the people and to say who moved first but Leper suddenly clams up. He becomes suspicious and declares that he will not incriminate himself. As Brinker tries to bring Leper back to his senses, Finny rises and declares that he doesn't care what happened. He then rushes out of the room in tears. The boys hear his footsteps and the tapping of his cane as he runs down the hall, followed by the horrible sound of his body falling down the marble staircase.

Analysis

The snowball fight that greets Gene upon his arrival constitutes yet another example of what defines Finny: his anarchic vibrancy and his love of pure sport, free of winners and losers. Although the snowy chaos seems to testify to the durability of Finny's spirit, his power diminishes over the course of the chapter. First, the news about Leper's madness deals a fatal blow to Finny's fantasy that the war is a hoax. As long as it did not impinge upon their lives directly, Finny could go on telling himself—and Gene—that the war did not exist. Having seen the disturbed Leper, however, Finny cannot keep up the pretense any longer; the hard fact of Leper's madness makes the war too real. It is now Gene who tries to keep up appearances and sustain the illusion of the conspiracy theory even after Leper's madness shatters it. As long as the war lacks reality, Gene knows that he can be with Finny, since the fact that he can join the military while Finny cannot becomes irrelevant. Gene thus clings to Finny's fantasy until Finny himself destroys it—with a tone of irony all the more shattering in its departure from Finny's characteristic sincerity.

Brinker's visit to Gene and Finny's room occasions a physical description of the bedroom walls for the first time. We learn that Finny has hung a picture of Roosevelt and Churchill, representing, to him, the fat, old men who have created the war. More important, however, the description gives us new insight into Gene. Gene has hung a picture of a southern plantation, which, he notes, constitutes a "bald-faced lie," part of a false identity that he assumed when he first came to Devon. Although he is from the upper South, Gene recounts that he had initially faked an accent from a state far south of his own and given the impression that the sentimental photograph showed his house. This insight into Gene's prior deceit puts the reader on the alert; the picture of the plantation becomes a symbol of Gene's unreliability as a source of information about his own life, a symbol of his inability to come to terms with his own identity. We wonder how accurately Gene has narrated the scene of Finny's fall and the events surrounding it; like Brinker, we become increasingly suspicious.

The meaning of Finny's remark to Gene, amid discussion of Leper, that he needs to trust Gene and believe him because he knows Gene better than he knows anyone else is ambiguous. One can argue that Knowles is suggesting ironically how little Finny really knows Gene, that he is completely oblivious to Gene's earlier pettiness and Gene's role in his accident. One can also argue that Knowles is implying that Finny knows everything—that he simply chooses to overlook the evidence against Gene because of his extreme dependence on him and need to love him.

The issues touched upon in these scenes now emerge in full force with Brinker's makeshift trial. The trial scene constitutes the final victory of the winter session over the summer session, of Brinker's desire for truth and justice over Finny and Gene's desire to preserve innocence and keep reality at bay. Brinker clearly believes that he is doing the right thing; one can argue that he is serving the interests of an abstractly defined justice. But while justice is supposed to be blind, as Gene notes, the only thing to which Brinker seems blind is Finny's lack of interest in having the truth extracted. This shying away from discovery is obvious in the way Finny describes the events: he deliberately recounts that Gene was at the bottom of the tree in order to deflect guilt away from his friend. It is left to the half-mad Leper to tell what really happened and finally break down Finny's wall of denial. Again, we wonder about Leper's inner psychology and motives: "I'm important too," he tells the tribunal;

in a sense, he seems to be exacting his revenge on Finny and Gene for the closeness of their friendship and for the fact that he was not part of it.

Just as in the initial portrayal of the scene of Finny's fall, Gene's narration breaks down at the crucial moments. In the scene of the fall, the reader is given an account of the external steps leading to the disaster but not of the inner processes unfolding in Gene's mind. Similarly, when Brinker now interrogates the boys, Gene narrates the external facts of the scene but refuses to portray his reactions: we witness neither fear, nor anger, nor even resignation. Except for brief calculations about whether people will believe Leper, Gene treats the terribly important events going on around him with a bizarre lack of emotion. This quality compels us once again to ponder how reliable a narrator Gene is; we must continually question the accuracy of his portrayals and analyze the story for ourselves, reading between the lines.

CHAPTER 12

SUMMARY

In the moments following Finny's crash on the staircase, the boys behave with surprising presence of mind as they fetch the wrestling coach, who lives nearby, to give Finny first aid; they also send someone to Dr. Stanpole's house. Dr. Stanpole arrives and has Finny carried out on a chair. Dr. Stanpole tells Gene that Finny's leg is broken again but assures him that it is a much cleaner break than last time. The crowd of boys breaks up and Gene sneaks off to the infirmary to peek in and try to see what is going on. He sits outside in the dark, imagining Finny saying absurd things to the doctors and nurses, until finally the doctor and the other adults leave, turning out the light in Finny's room. Gene crawls up to the side of the building and opens the window. Finny recognizes him in the darkness and begins to struggle angrily in his bed, accusing Gene of coming to break something else in him. He falls out of bed, but Gene restrains himself from going into the room to help him back up. Gene tells Finny that he is sorry and then leaves.

All through the night, Gene wanders the campus, thinking that he can see a new level of meaning in everything around him and feeling that he himself is nothing but a meaningless dream, a "roaming ghost." He falls asleep under the stadium, imagining that its walls can speak, that they can say powerful things, but that he, as a ghost, cannot hear them. The next morning, he returns to his room before class and finds a note from Dr. Stanpole asking him to bring some of Finny's things to the infirmary. Gene packs Finny's suitcase and brings it to him. Finny's voice betrays no emotion, but as he looks through the suitcase, Gene sees that his hands are shaking. Finny tells Gene that all winter he has been writing to various military branches all over the allied world, begging to be allowed to enlist but that all of them have rejected him because of his leg. He says that the reason he kept telling Gene that there was no war was that he could not be a part of it. Gene tells Finny that he would never have been any good in the war anyway because he would have gone over to the other side and made friends and gotten everyone confused about whom they were fighting.

Finny bursts into tears and says that some sort of blind impulse must have seized Gene on the tree those many months ago, that he hadn't known what he was doing. He asks Gene to confirm that it was some impulse, not some deep feeling against Finny, that took hold of him that day; Gene answers that some "ignorance" or "crazy thing" inside him made him jostle the limb. Finny assures him that he understands and believes Gene. The doctor tells Gene that he is going to set the bone this afternoon; Gene can come back that evening after Finny comes out of the anesthesia. Gene goes about his day mechanically and comes back to the infirmary at the appointed time. Dr. Stanpole finds him in the hall outside Finny's room and tells him that Finny is dead. As Gene listens numbly, the doctor explains that a bit of marrow escaped from the bone as he was setting it, entering Finny's bloodstream and stopping his heart. Gene doesn't cry, not even later at Finny's funeral. He feels that, in some way, it is his own funeral as well.

ANALYSIS

Gene's nighttime wanderings lead him to a tragic realization. As he floats aimlessly, he comes to recognize that he has no sense of himself, no sense of his own identity or being. Gene has spent so much of the novel losing himself in Finny that, once severed from him, he feels himself to be a ghost, departed from the world of the living. This spectral existence renders him deaf to the profound lessons that his world has to teach him; it cuts him off from a meaningful life. Thus, he tells us that the landscape "speaks" to him but that he cannot hear its messages.

It is difficult to know what to make of the interaction between the two friends on the following day. At night, when Gene comes to Finny's window, Finny lashes out at him; but the next day, Finny is ready to forgive, ready to believe that what happened on the branch arose from a sudden, uncontrollable urge that Gene could not control—that it had nothing to do with their friendship. The reader is left uncertain as to whether Finny really believes this idea or is simply forcing himself to believe. If he were to believe that Gene really harbored some deep resentment toward him, he would have to give up Gene's friendship, a prospect that he considers too painful. Similarly, when Gene eagerly joins Finny in attributing the jounce to blind impulse, we are left to question the extent to which he believes this idea. Again, Gene, ever the problematic narrator, withholds information: he tells us what he says to Finny, but characteristically, he does not tell us his thoughts.

Ultimately, by refusing to resolve the matter definitively, the novel forces the reader to contemplate the subtleties of the story. That is, unable to determine the truth behind Finny's fall, we must base considerations of Gene's seeming guilt on other elements. His mindset prior to the fall—his feelings of rivalry and envy—would seem to render Gene guilty regardless of whether or not he consciously jostled the branch. For example, if he wished for harm to come to Finny, even if not at the specific moment in the tree, then this malevolent intention would cost him our trust and lead us to believe that he might well have been responsible for the accident. Gene's devotion to Finny after the accident, however, would seem to exonerate him. On the other hand, one can argue that this devotion arises out of Gene's deep shame, which may itself be considered in various lights. His shame seems to point to his guilt, yet perhaps his intense regret and self-hatred have sufficed as atonement for his misdeed.

The strange manner of Finny's death seems to suggest a fundamental flaw in the codependency that marks his relationship with Gene. Gene and Finny rely on each other to deal with the anxieties of adolescence and the encroaching war and seem to need each other in order to survive. Their relationship allows them to reinforce for each other the self-delusion that the war is a conspiracy, that the Olympics will take place as usual, that they need never grow up and face reality. The blurring of their identities into a haven of blitheness and Olympic glory against the tribulations that they know await them prevents them from properly navigating the difficulties of adolescence and maturing into adulthood. For Finny, the implications of this failure to gain a more astute understanding of the world are tragic. He is never able to understand that, unlike him, other people do have enemies and are not always content. One can argue that the stray bit of marrow that plugs Finny's heart symbolizes Gene's underlying resentment toward the unsuspecting Finny—a resentment that permeates his desire to be a part of Finny.

Gene's reflections on Finny's death suggest that, whether or not the friends' intense bond actually causes Finny's death, the bond between them will last beyond death. In the moment of Finny's passing, the boys are symbolically still a part of each other. Gene himself recognizes this fact, as evident from his remark that Finny's funeral feels like his own. In a sense, the funeral is his own. Gene is merged with Finny to so great an extent that it is difficult to imagine one boy continuing to exist without the other.

Chapter 13

> [M]y war ended before I ever put on a uniform . . . I
> killed my enemy [at school]. Only . . . Phineas never
> hated anyone. . . .
>
> *(See* QUOTATIONS, *p. 57)*

Summary

The school year draws to a close, and Gene's class graduates. The school donates its Far Common quadrangle to the military for a parachute riggers' school. Gene watches from his window as the army drives in at the beginning of summer to occupy it. Brinker takes Gene down to the Butt Room to meet his father, who expresses his wish that he were younger, so that he could fight in the war. He chokes back his distaste at hearing Gene's plans to avoid the danger of the infantry by joining the navy and Brinker's decision to join the coast guard. He lectures them on the importance of serving their country honorably, saying that their lives will be defined in large part by what they do in the war. He leaves, and Brinker apologizes for his father's attitude, denouncing the older generation for causing the war and then expecting the younger generation to fight it. He goes to finish packing and Gene walks to the gym to clean out his locker. He finds a platoon of parachute riggers in the locker room and watches the men as they prepare to go to the playing fields to do calisthenics. Gene knows that he will soon take part in the same sort of regimentation, but he is glad that it will not take place for him at Devon.

Gene now speaks again from the perspective of his older self. He says that he never killed anyone during his time in the military—that his war was fought at Devon and that it was there that he killed his enemy. Everyone, he says, finds themselves pitted violently against something in the world at some point in their lives; everyone realizes that there is something in the world that is hostile to them, and they are never the same after that realization. For his classmates, Gene says—for Brinker and Leper and Quackenbush—this realization came with the war. Each found ways of defending himself against it, by either adopting a stance of careless unconcern, descending into insanity, or treating others with a bullying anger. Only Finny, Gene reflects, never sensed the existence of an enemy to fight; thus it was that Finny was never afraid and never hated anyone. Finny alone, he muses, understood that the perceived enemy might not be an enemy at all.

ANALYSIS

The novel ends on an appropriately dark note, as the war invades Devon. Although the characters have felt the war descending upon the school throughout the book, the incursion is literal this time, as soldiers set up camp on the campus. However, for Gene and his classmates, the abstract notions that one would expect to accompany the war—honor and glory—have drained away, leaving only an adolescent cynicism. Those leaving Devon for the army make fun of the parachute riggers, whose sewing machines make them seem slightly absurd, even as the boys themselves make plans to do whatever is necessary to avoid active combat. Even Brinker, who had wanted to enlist early on, has now decided to join the coast guard, which will keep him a safe distance from any real action. Everyone now unconsciously echoes Finny's belief that the war is a conspiracy of the old against the young, and they resolve not to be "taken in." Brinker's father, with his talk of pride and duty and serving one's country, seems indeed to personify Finny's fat, old men, which Brinker and the others are quick to recognize. "He and his crowd are responsible for [the war]!" Brinker declares. "And we're going to fight it!"

Brinker expresses the general disillusionment of his classmates, a disillusion that has stemmed partly from their knowledge of Leper's fate, partly from their despair over Finny's death, and partly from the fear associated with the end of the waiting period and beginning of their real involvement in the war. But Gene, in these final pages, does not share in the boys' disillusionment, for he has achieved a higher insight. Due to the narrative structure of the novel, it is difficult to discern whether Gene first comes to these understandings during the time period narrated or whether he only now, older, arrives at them. In any case, the narrating Gene now explains the insight that has allowed him to understand the war as something deeper and more firmly rooted in the human condition. To Gene, war is not merely the expression of a few old men's selfishness; rather, war emerges out of a profound and toxic ignorance in the human heart—an ignorance that causes one to seek out an enemy and to see the world as a hostile place.

Gene thus introduces the final metaphorical meaning of the novel's wartime backdrop: World War II represents man's need for a personal war—for a personal enemy—to defend against and kill. Part of growing up, Gene suggests, involves finding this enemy and losing one's childhood illusion that the world is a fundamentally friendly place. He goes through the list of characters and discusses how each has reacted to this discovery of the "enemy": Mr. Ludsbury with arrogant disdain; Brinker with resentment; Leper with a surrender to madness. Although Gene doesn't include himself on this list, the reader remembers his earlier statement that he killed his enemy while at Devon: the implication, of course, is that Finny was the focus of his hatred, the enemy in his private war. The precise reason for this enmity is never fully explained; nevertheless, from the story as a whole we may conclude that it was quite a perverse hatred. For it stemmed not from Gene's jealousy of his friend's accomplishments but rather from his jealousy of Finny's goodness and innocence.

The novel closes with Gene reflecting on Finny's great gift—his ability to remain innocent ("unfallen," one might say), see the world as a good, beneficent place, and never even imagine the possibility of an enemy. The book's last lines leave us to wonder if Finny's worldview—if what we consider the enemy is only a fabrication of some profound ignorance in mankind's inner being—is ultimately truer than that of the other characters. For if our hatred of others stems from something intrinsic to the human heart, then sincere friendships and peaceful societies will always be imperiled. If, on the other hand, our animosities stem from ignorance, then perhaps we may retain hope for our futures, both as individuals and as communities. Perhaps we may have reason to hope that, given enough experience and reflection, we may become better human beings.

Important Quotations Explained

1.   I found it. I found a single sustaining thought. The thought was, You and Phineas are even already. You are even in enmity. You are both coldly driving ahead for yourselves alone. . . . I felt better. Yes, I sensed it like the sweat of relief when nausea passes away; I felt better. We were even after all, even in enmity. The deadly rivalry was on both sides after all.

This quotation is from Chapter 4, as Gene slowly becomes conscious of the tremendous resentment and envy that he feels toward Finny, who is a far superior athlete, has a much stronger personality, and can talk his way out of any trouble. We see Gene develop a strategy for coping with this resentment: he tells himself that Finny feels exactly the same way, convincing himself that just as he envies Finny's athleticism so must Finny envy Gene's academic achievements. This vision of a "deadly rivalry" between himself and Finny sustains Gene for some time; it enables him to avoid feeling shame about his resentment toward Finny and drives him to excel academically in order to spite his friend. Yet the vision is only temporary: after he realizes that Finny shares neither his sense of competition nor his resentment, Gene sinks into a jealousy more bitter than before, convinced of Finny's moral superiority as well. It is in the shadow of this second envy that Finny's fall takes place.

2.   He had never been jealous of me for a second. Now I knew
     that there never was and never could have been any rivalry
     between us. I was not of the same quality as he. I couldn't
     stand this. . . . Holding firmly to the trunk, I took a step
     toward him, and then my knees bent and I jounced the
     limb. Finny, his balance gone, swung his head around to
     look at me for an instant with extreme interest, and then
     he tumbled sideways, broke through the little branches
     below and hit the bank with a sickening, unnatural thud.
     It was the first clumsy physical action I had ever seen him
     make. With unthinking sureness I moved out on the limb
     and jumped into the river, every trace of my fear of this
     forgotten.

These lines encompass the climax of the novel, at the end of Chapter
4, when Gene shakes the tree limb and makes Finny fall. In the moments leading up to this scene, Gene's notion of a mutual enmity and
competition between himself and Finny breaks down as he realizes
that Finny has never wanted to compete with anyone—certainly not
with him. "I was not of the same quality as he," Gene says, suddenly
perceiving his own moral inferiority to his best friend. His anguish
at this realization ("I couldn't stand this") is the only explanation
offered for the events on the tree, which are described in a detached
tone, without allowing us access to Gene's thoughts as his knees bend
and the limb shakes. By refusing to tell us what he is thinking, Gene
leaves the question of his guilt up in the air. Indeed, he refuses to say
anything—perhaps because he himself is not sure about the degree of
his guilt. In a story that is largely about the dangers of being codependent and identifying too closely with another person, it is apt that we
must consider the fall for ourselves, without Gene's insight.

Gene's comment that Finny's slip from the branch is "the first
clumsy physical action I had ever seen him make" marks the fall as
the first sign in the novel of Finny's mortality. Up until the fall, Finny
has reigned supreme as the epitome of charm and grace; never de-
feated in athletics, he talks his way out of predicaments with teachers and maintains a blithe, untroubled existence, seeming to glide
along in life. Finny's fall is thus a literal fall from grace; he is no
longer the physical paragon that Gene earlier considers him, and his
death is clumsy—both the tripping down the stairs and the stopping
of his heart by a piece of bone marrow.

3.   "Listen, pal, if I can't play sports, you're going to play
      them for me," and I lost part of myself to him then, and a
      soaring sense of freedom revealed that this must have been
      my purpose from the first: to become a part of Phineas.

At the end of Chapter 6, Gene records this telephone conversation
with Finny, in which the recuperating Finny expresses horror at the
thought of Gene fulfilling his athletic requirement by managing the
crew team. Their conversation establishes a pattern for their post-
accident relationship, in which Gene, purged of his animosity and
resentment, increasingly begins to blur the line between himself and
his friend. He allows Finny to live through him, becoming "a part
of Phineas" by letting Finny train him to be the athlete that Finny
can no longer be. But even as Finny lives through Gene, Gene is
clearly living through Finny; for, as his words here suggest, to experience life through Finny is to accrue a sense of "purpose" and a
sense of self, both of which Gene had previously lacked. The friends'
codependency, which develops as Finny trains Gene for his fantasy
"1944 Olympics," fulfills deep needs on both sides: Finny's need to
live out his dreams of athletic glory and Gene's desire to escape his
identity. Thus, each boy, by becoming "part" of the other, protects
himself from reality—Finny from his sudden but permanent physical shortcomings and Gene from his moral shortcomings.

QUOTATIONS

4.   Fear seized my stomach like a cramp. I didn't care what I
     said to him now; it was myself I was worried about. For
     if Leper was psycho it was the army which had done it to
     him, and I and all of us were on the brink of the army.

This quotation comes from Chapter 10, when Gene goes to Vermont
to visit Leper, who has deserted the army after suffering hallucinations. In Leper's home, Gene listens to him recount the story of his
training camp madness, and grows distraught—not, we quickly
realize, for Leper's sake, but for his own. For Gene, Leper's transformation from gentle nature-lover into verified "psycho" shatters
the illusion, foisted on him by Finny, that they can stave off adulthood forever. Gene earlier joins with his classmates in celebrating
imagined heroics performed by Leper; they try to cover up their own
insecurities about military service by naïvely pretending that their
meek classmate is succeeding mightily as a soldier. Now, however,
seeing that army life has, in fact, made Leper a "psycho," Gene can
regard the war only with great fear. In the minds of Gene and the
rest of the boys, Leper's madness transforms the war from a distant
threat into an immediate reality.

5. I never killed anybody and I never developed an intense
    level of hatred for the enemy. Because my war ended before
    I ever put on a uniform; I was on active duty all my time at
    school; I killed my enemy there. Only Phineas never was
    afraid, only Phineas never hated anyone.

These words are among Gene's final musings in the novel, as he reflects on the meaning of his experiences at Devon and then in the war. He suggests that every human being, at a certain point in his or her life, decides that the world is a fundamentally hostile place and subsequently finds enemies to fight with and kill. He believes that for most of his classmates, this moment came with fighting in World War II, with real enemies—but for himself, it came before the onset of military violence or the arrival of army-issued weapons; Gene fought his war while still at Devon. Gene does not detail who his "enemy" was, and we are left to decide for ourselves whether he refers to Finny or to his own inner demons. In either case, he goes on to say that what separated Finny from everyone else was his inability, or lack of desire, to understand these notions of war and enmity. For Finny, everyone was a friend; no one deserved fear and hatred. This innocence contributed to a moral superiority in Finny; but it also led to his destruction, the novel suggests, because it rendered him unable to anticipate, and cope with, the revelation of betrayal.

QUOTATIONS

KEY FACTS

FULL TITLE
  A Separate Peace

AUTHOR
  John Knowles

TYPE OF WORK
  Novel

GENRE
  Coming-of-age story; tragedy

LANGUAGE
  English

TIME AND PLACE WRITTEN
  New England, 1957–1958

DATE OF FIRST PUBLICATION
  1959

PUBLISHER
  Macmillan

NARRATOR
  Gene Forrester narrates the story as he revisits his high school campus and recalls events that happened fifteen years earlier.

POINT OF VIEW
  The narrator speaks in the first person, describing events as he perceived them at the time of their occurrence, though occasionally with the augmented knowledge of hindsight (sometimes it is difficult to distinguish between the perspective of the younger Gene and the older Gene). Although he apparently recounts external events with honesty and thoroughness, Gene is an unreliable narrator in that he withholds his own thoughts and emotions regarding certain crucial scenes, such as Finny's fall and the boys' makeshift trial of Gene.

TONE

Occasionally nostalgic but largely brooding and melancholy; often regretful

TENSE

Past tense; the narrator refers to the recent past ("not long ago") before launching into a flashback on the more remote past of fifteen years earlier. The book then ends with a return to the recent past.

SETTING (TIME)

The story begins in 1958 but quickly flashes back to the years 1942–1943

SETTING (PLACE)

The Devon School, an exclusive New England academy

PROTAGONIST

Gene

MAJOR CONFLICT

Gene feels both love and hate for his best friend, Finny, worshipping and resenting Finny's athletic and moral superiorities.

RISING ACTION

Gene's envy of Finny grows; Gene realizes that Finny doesn't return his resentment; Gene becomes jealous of Finny's seeming incapacity to be envious; Gene feels that Finny is a morally superior person; Finny suggests that the boys climb a tree together.

CLIMAX

Gene jounces the limb of the tree, making Finny fall and shatter his leg.

FALLING ACTION

Gene feels guilty about Finny's fall; he and Finny become even more intimate, developing a codependency; the boys put Gene on "trial" for the accident; Finny falls down the stairs and breaks his leg again; Finny dies during the operation on his leg.

THEMES

Codependency's threat to identity; the creation of inner enemies

MOTIFS

Transformation; athletics

SYMBOLS

World War II; the summer and winter sessions at Devon;
Finny's fall

FORESHADOWING

Prior to his flashback, the older Gene makes reference to a
"death by violence" and to fears that he had at school, which
are associated with a flight of marble steps and a tree. These
remarks foreshadow Gene's revelation of Finny's two accidents:
the falling from the tree and the falling down the steps.

STUDY QUESTIONS

1. *To what extent should we consider Gene to be an unreliable narrator? How does this concern affect our understanding of the story that he tells and our attitude toward him?*

A *Separate Peace* is a novel told entirely in flashback, by a narrator—Gene Forrester—who is our only source of information regarding the events that he recounts. As the story develops, the initial trust that exists between reader and narrator gradually frays, as we realize that Gene, while probably not lying about the events of the story, is clearly withholding information about his own motivations for, or reactions to, the deeds of himself and others. This reservation is apparent in the way that he talks about his friendship with Finny in the first few chapters: though Gene initially declares Finny to be his best friend and claims that he is neither jealous nor resentful of the charismatic athlete, it soon becomes clear, through subtle asides and various inconsistent behaviors, that the relationship is actually marked by forceful envy and even hatred. When Finny and Gene illicitly spend the night at the beach, for example, Finny declares his happiness in the two boys' friendship; Gene, however, makes no such utterance.

At critical moments in the story, Gene simply describes external events without revealing his thoughts, emotions, and motivations. This disturbing lack permeates the climax of the novel, and we wait in vain for the narrator to tell us what passed through his head prior to and during the terrible moment of Finny's fall. Similarly, Gene's narration becomes dispassionate at the makeshift trial when it becomes clear that his secret crime will be revealed. Thus, throughout the novel, even as Gene is theoretically opening up to the reader, an important part of him remains sealed off.

Gene's status as an unreliable narrator creates a problem of sympathy that persists throughout the novel. Because it is Gene's perspective through which we see the story, Gene is the character with whom the reader most closely identifies. Yet, in his refusal to explain himself or the emotions and reasoning behind his perspective, he remains beyond our understanding, making it difficult for us to give him our wholehearted sympathy. Whether or not we think Gene has deliberately caused Finny's fall, we begin to feel increasingly alienated from him. Thus, even as we become ever more invested in the story's outcome, we become distrustful of its narrator.

2. *Discuss the relationship between codependency and identity in* A SEPARATE PEACE *and how these concepts help define the relationship between Gene and Finny.*

Early on in the novel, Gene's relationship to Finny seems to be defined by simple envy. Finny is athletic and quick-tongued, with a powerful and assertive spirit; Gene feels overshadowed and even controlled by his friend. After Finny's fall, however, Gene seems to be purged of his animosity and resentment, and he begins to blur the line between himself and his friend. Just before knocking Finny out of the tree, he seems to realize that Finny is his moral superior. Over the course of the rest of the novel, he tries to escape his own, pettier self by losing himself in Finny. The post-accident scene, in which Gene rather bizarrely dresses in his friend's clothes and, looking in the mirror, finds contentment in the notion that he looks exactly like Finny, symbolizes this attempted merging of identities. In allowing Finny to train him to be the athlete that Finny himself can no longer be, Gene seems to be letting Finny live through him. Yet, just as Finny lives through Gene, Gene lives through Finny by letting Finny's identity overwhelm his own. Thus, the two exist in a codependent state, each needing the other. Soon they share the same dreams and illusions: that the Olympics will proceed in 1944 as usual and that the war is merely a conspiracy; they thus live amid a "separate peace." The more time goes by and the more the war encroaches upon Devon, the more the boys depend upon each other to maintain this fantasy. Ultimately, then, while this codependency allows the boys to remain content and feel secure, it hampers their entrance into the reality of adulthood. So, too, does it limit their development as individuals in touch with their own individual identities. This codependency may be unhealthy, even destructive, as the bizarre manner of Finny's death—the fatal penetration of bone marrow into the heart—seems to suggest.

3.   *How does World War II function in the novel on a symbolic and thematic level? How does it relate to the title of the book?*

The war constitutes a looming presence throughout the novel, constantly pressing in on Devon and drawing closer to the boys. Its symbolic meanings are numerous: it represents a loss of innocence, the coming of adulthood, and, most important, the way that human beings, out of ignorance, regard the world as a hostile place and look for enemies where none exist. Each character, the narrator suggests at the end of the novel, creates an enemy for himself and deals with that enemy in various ways. Leper's reaction to the enemy is to lose himself in madness; Brinker copes by assuming a bravado and insisting upon order; Gene, too, fights a private war—against Finny and his own dark nature. Finny alone does not see enemies everywhere; he is enamored with peace and creates the "separate peace" of the title for himself. The summer session is one such innocent peacetime, when the war still seems far away. After his injury, however, Finny is forced to find a sense of peace in denial, by pretending that the war is just a hoax. The "separate" quality of Finny's peace stems from his unwillingness to conceive of an enemy and Gene's inability to join him in this peace because he cannot wholly dispel his envy toward, and resentment of, Finny.

How to Write
Literary Analysis

The Literary Essay: A Step-by-Step Guide

When you read for pleasure, your only goal is enjoyment. You might find yourself reading to get caught up in an exciting story, to learn about an interesting time or place, or just to pass time. Maybe you're looking for inspiration, guidance, or a reflection of your own life. There are as many different, valid ways of reading a book as there are books in the world.

When you read a work of literature in an English class, however, you're being asked to read in a special way: you're being asked to perform *literary analysis*. To analyze something means to break it down into smaller parts and then examine how those parts work, both individually and together. Literary analysis involves examining all the parts of a novel, play, short story, or poem—elements such as character, setting, tone, and imagery—and thinking about how the author uses those elements to create certain effects.

A literary essay isn't a book review: you're not being asked whether or not you liked a book or whether you'd recommend it to another reader. A literary essay also isn't like the kind of book report you wrote when you were younger, where your teacher wanted you to summarize the book's action. A high school- or college-level literary essay asks, "How does this piece of literature actually work?" "How does it do what it does?" and, "Why might the author have made the choices he or she did?"

The Seven Steps
No one is born knowing how to analyze literature; it's a skill you learn and a process you can master. As you gain more practice with this kind of thinking and writing, you'll be able to craft a method that works best for you. But until then, here are seven basic steps to writing a well-constructed literary essay:

> *1. Ask questions*
> *2. Collect evidence*
> *3. Construct a thesis*

4. Develop and organize arguments
5. Write the introduction
6. Write the body paragraphs
7. Write the conclusion

---

1. Ask Questions

When you're assigned a literary essay in class, your teacher will often provide you with a list of writing prompts. Lucky you! Now all you have to do is choose one. Do yourself a favor and pick a topic that interests you. You'll have a much better (not to mention easier) time if you start off with something you enjoy thinking about. If you are asked to come up with a topic by yourself, though, you might start to feel a little panicked. Maybe you have too many ideas—or none at all. Don't worry. Take a deep breath and start by asking yourself these questions:

- **What struck you?** Did a particular image, line, or scene linger in your mind for a long time? If it fascinated you, chances are you can draw on it to write a fascinating essay.

- **What confused you?** Maybe you were surprised to see a character act in a certain way, or maybe you didn't understand why the book ended the way it did. Confusing moments in a work of literature are like a loose thread in a sweater: if you pull on it, you can unravel the entire thing. Ask yourself why the author chose to write about that character or scene the way he or she did and you might tap into some important insights about the work as a whole.

- **Did you notice any patterns?** Is there a phrase that the main character uses constantly or an image that repeats throughout the book? If you can figure out how that pattern weaves through the work and what the significance of that pattern is, you've almost got your entire essay mapped out.

- **Did you notice any contradictions or ironies?** Great works of literature are complex; great literary essays recognize and explain those complexities. Maybe the title (*Happy Days*) totally disagrees with the book's subject matter (hungry orphans dying in the woods). Maybe the main character acts one way around his family and a completely different way around his friends and associates. If you can find a way to explain a work's contradictory elements, you've got the seeds of a great essay.

At this point, you don't need to know exactly what you're going to say about your topic; you just need a place to begin your exploration. You can help direct your reading and brainstorming by formulating your topic as a *question*, which you'll then try to answer in your essay. The best questions invite critical debates and discussions, not just a rehashing of the summary. Remember, you're looking for something you can *prove or argue* based on evidence you find in the text. Finally, remember to keep the scope of your question in mind: is this a topic you can adequately address within the word or page limit you've been given? Conversely, is this a topic big enough to fill the required length?

GOOD QUESTIONS

> *"Are Romeo and Juliet's parents responsible for the deaths of their children?"*
> *"Why do pigs keep showing up in* LORD OF THE FLIES*?"*
> *"Are Dr. Frankenstein and his monster alike? How?"*

BAD QUESTIONS

> *"What happens to Scout in* TO KILL A MOCKINGBIRD*?"*
> *"What do the other characters in* JULIUS CAESAR *think about Caesar?"*
> *"How does Hester Prynne in* THE SCARLET LETTER *remind me of my sister?"*

---

2. COLLECT EVIDENCE

Once you know what question you want to answer, it's time to scour the book for things that will help you answer the question. Don't worry if you don't know what you want to say yet—right now you're just collecting ideas and material and letting it all percolate. Keep track of passages, symbols, images, or scenes that deal with your topic. Eventually, you'll start making connections between these examples and your thesis will emerge.

Here's a brief summary of the various parts that compose each and every work of literature. These are the elements that you will analyze in your essay, and which you will offer as evidence to support your arguments. For more on the parts of literary works, see the Glossary of Literary Terms at the end of this section.

ELEMENTS OF STORY   These are the *what*s of the work—what happens, where it happens, and to whom it happens.

- **Plot:** All of the events and actions of the work.
- **Character:** The people who act and are acted upon in a literary work. The main character of a work is known as the *protagonist.*
- **Conflict:** The central tension in the work. In most cases, the protagonist wants something, while opposing forces (antagonists) hinder the protagonist's progress.
- **Setting:** When and where the work takes place. Elements of setting include location, time period, time of day, weather, social atmosphere, and economic conditions.
- **Narrator:** The person telling the story. The narrator may straightforwardly report what happens, convey the subjective opinions and perceptions of one or more characters, or provide commentary and opinion in his or her own voice.
- **Themes:** The main idea or message of the work—usually an abstract idea about people, society, or life in general. A work may have many themes, which may be in tension with one another.

ELEMENTS OF STYLE   These are the *how*s—how the characters speak, how the story is constructed, and how language is used throughout the work.

- **Structure and organization:** How the parts of the work are assembled. Some novels are narrated in a linear, chronological fashion, while others skip around in time. Some plays follow a traditional three- or five-act structure, while others are a series of loosely connected scenes. Some authors deliberately leave gaps in their works, leaving readers to puzzle out the missing information. A work's structure and organization can tell you a lot about the kind of message it wants to convey.
- **Point of view:** The perspective from which a story is told. In *first-person point of view,* the narrator involves him or herself in the story. ("I went to the store"; "We watched in horror as the bird slammed into the window.") A first-person narrator is usually the protagonist of the work, but not always. In *third-person point of view,* the narrator does not participate

in the story. A third-person narrator may closely follow a specific character, recounting that individual character's thoughts or experiences, or it may be what we call an *omniscient* narrator. Omniscient narrators see and know all: they can witness any event in any time or place and are privy to the inner thoughts and feelings of all characters. Remember that the narrator and the author are not the same thing!

- **Diction:** Word choice. Whether a character uses dry, clinical language or flowery prose with lots of exclamation points can tell you a lot about his or her attitude and personality.

- **Syntax:** Word order and sentence construction. Syntax is a crucial part of establishing an author's narrative voice. Ernest Hemingway, for example, is known for writing in very short, straightforward sentences, while James Joyce characteristically wrote in long, incredibly complicated lines.

- **Tone:** The mood or feeling of the text. Diction and syntax often contribute to the tone of a work. A novel written in short, clipped sentences that use small, simple words might feel brusque, cold, or matter-of-fact.

- **Imagery:** Language that appeals to the senses, representing things that can be seen, smelled, heard, tasted, or touched.

- **Figurative language:** Language that is not meant to be interpreted literally. The most common types of figurative language are *metaphors* and *similes,* which compare two unlike things in order to suggest a similarity between them— for example, "All the world's a stage," or "The moon is like a ball of green cheese." (Metaphors say one thing *is* another thing; similes claim that one thing is *like* another thing.)

---

3. CONSTRUCT A THESIS

When you've examined all the evidence you've collected and know how you want to answer the question, it's time to write your thesis statement. A *thesis* is a claim about a work of literature that needs to be supported by evidence and arguments. The thesis statement is the heart of the literary essay, and the bulk of your paper will be spent trying to prove this claim. A good thesis will be:

- **Arguable.** "*The Great Gatsby* describes New York society in the 1920s" isn't a thesis—it's a fact.

- **Provable through textual evidence**. "*Hamlet* is a confusing but ultimately very well-written play" is a weak thesis because it offers the writer's personal opinion about the book. Yes, it's arguable, but it's not a claim that can be proved or supported with examples taken from the play itself.

- **Surprising**. "Both George and Lenny change a great deal in *Of Mice and Men*" is a weak thesis because it's obvious. A really strong thesis will argue for a reading of the text that is not immediately apparent.

- **Specific**. "Dr. Frankenstein's monster tells us a lot about the human condition" is *almost* a really great thesis statement, but it's still too vague. What does the writer mean by "a lot"? *How* does the monster tell us so much about the human condition?

Good Thesis Statements

Question: In *Romeo and Juliet*, which is more powerful in shaping the lovers' story: fate or foolishness?

Thesis: "Though Shakespeare defines Romeo and Juliet as 'star-crossed lovers' and images of stars and planets appear throughout the play, a closer examination of that celestial imagery reveals that the stars are merely witnesses to the characters' foolish activities and not the causes themselves."

Question: How does the bell jar function as a symbol in Sylvia Plath's *The Bell Jar*?

Thesis: "A bell jar is a bell-shaped glass that has three basic uses: to hold a specimen for observation, to contain gases, and to maintain a vacuum. The bell jar appears in each of these capacities in *The Bell Jar*, Plath's semi-autobiographical novel, and each appearance marks a different stage in Esther's mental breakdown."

Question: Would Piggy in *The Lord of the Flies* make a good island leader if he were given the chance?

Thesis: "Though the intelligent, rational, and innovative Piggy has the mental characteristics of a good leader, he ultimately lacks the social skills necessary to be an effective one. Golding emphasizes this point by giving Piggy a foil in the charismatic Jack, whose magnetic personality allows him to capture and wield power effectively, if not always wisely."

4. Develop and Organize Arguments

The reasons and examples that support your thesis will form the middle paragraphs of your essay. Since you can't really write your thesis statement until you know how you'll structure your argument, you'll probably end up working on steps 3 and 4 at the same time.

There's no single method of argumentation that will work in every context. One essay prompt might ask you to compare and contrast two characters, while another asks you to trace an image through a given work of literature. These questions require different kinds of answers and therefore different kinds of arguments. Below, we'll discuss three common kinds of essay prompts and some strategies for constructing a solid, well-argued case.

Types of Literary Essays

- **Compare and contrast**

  Compare and contrast the characters of Huck and Jim in The Adventures of Huckleberry Finn.

  Chances are you've written this kind of essay before. In an academic literary context, you'll organize your arguments the same way you would in any other class. You can either go *subject by subject* or *point by point*. In the former, you'll discuss one character first and then the second. In the latter, you'll choose several traits (attitude toward life, social status, images and metaphors associated with the character) and devote a paragraph to each. You may want to use a mix of these two approaches—for example, you may want to spend a paragraph a piece broadly sketching Huck's and Jim's personalities before transitioning into a paragraph or two that describes a few key points of comparison. This can be a highly effective strategy if you want to make a counterintuitive argument—that, despite seeming to be totally different, the two objects being compared are actually similar in a very important way (or vice versa). Remember that your essay should reveal something fresh or unexpected about the text, so think beyond the obvious parallels and differences.

- **Trace**

  Choose an image—for example, birds, knives, or eyes—and trace that image throughout Macbeth.

  Sounds pretty easy, right? All you need to do is read the play, underline every appearance of a knife in *Macbeth,* and then list them in your essay in the order they appear, right? Well, not exactly. Your teacher doesn't want a simple catalog of examples. He or she wants to see you make *connections* between those examples—that's the difference between summarizing and analyzing. In the *Macbeth* example above, think about the different contexts in which knives appear in the play and to what effect. In *Macbeth*, there are real knives and imagined knives; knives that kill and knives that simply threaten. Categorize and classify your examples to give them some order. Finally, always keep the overall effect in mind. After you choose and analyze your examples, you should come to some greater understanding about the work, as well as your chosen image, symbol, or phrase's role in developing the major themes and stylistic strategies of that work.

- **Debate**

  Is the society depicted in 1984 *good for its citizens?*

  In this kind of essay, you're being asked to debate a moral, ethical, or aesthetic issue regarding the work. You might be asked to judge a character or group of characters (*Is Caesar responsible for his own demise?*) or the work itself (*Is* JANE EYRE *a feminist novel?*). For this kind of essay, there are two important points to keep in mind. First, don't simply base your arguments on your personal feelings and reactions. Every literary essay expects you to read and analyze the work, so search for evidence in the text. What do characters in *1984* have to say about the government of Oceania? What images does Orwell use that might give you a hint about his attitude toward the government? As in any debate, you also need to make sure that you define all the necessary terms before you begin to argue your case. What does it mean to be a "good" society? What makes a novel "feminist"? You should define your terms right up front, in the first paragraph after your introduction.

  Second, remember that strong literary essays make contrary and surprising arguments. Try to think outside the box. In the *1984* example above, it seems like the obvious answer would be no, the totalitarian society depicted in Orwell's novel is *not* good for its citizens. But can you think of any arguments for the opposite side? Even if your final assertion is that the novel depicts a cruel, repressive, and therefore harmful society, acknowledging and responding to the counterargument will strengthen your overall case.

5. WRITE THE INTRODUCTION

Your introduction sets up the entire essay. It's where you present your topic and articulate the particular issues and questions you'll be addressing. It's also where you, as the writer, introduce yourself to your readers. A persuasive literary essay immediately establishes its writer as a knowledgeable, authoritative figure.

An introduction can vary in length depending on the overall length of the essay, but in a traditional five-paragraph essay it should be no longer than one paragraph. However long it is, your introduction needs to:

- **Provide any necessary context.** Your introduction should situate the reader and let him or her know what to expect. What book are you discussing? Which characters? What topic will you be addressing?

- **Answer the "So what?" question.** Why is this topic important, and why is your particular position on the topic noteworthy? Ideally, your introduction should pique the reader's interest by suggesting how your argument is surprising or otherwise counterintuitive. Literary essays make unexpected connections and reveal less-than-obvious truths.

- **Present your thesis.** This usually happens at or very near the end of your introduction.

- **Indicate the shape of the essay to come.** Your reader should finish reading your introduction with a good sense of the scope of your essay as well as the path you'll take toward proving your thesis. You don't need to spell out every step, but you do need to suggest the organizational pattern you'll be using.

Your introduction should not:

- **Be vague.** Beware of the two killer words in literary analysis: *interesting* and *important*. Of course the work, question, or example is interesting and important—that's why you're writing about it!

- **Open with any grandiose assertions.** Many student readers think that beginning their essays with a flamboyant statement such as, "Since the dawn of time, writers have been fascinated with the topic of free will," makes them

sound important and commanding. You know what? It
actually sounds pretty amateurish.

- **Wildly praise the work.** Another typical mistake student
  writers make is extolling the work or author. Your teacher
  doesn't need to be told that "Shakespeare is perhaps the
  greatest writer in the English language." You can mention
  a work's reputation in passing—by referring to *The Adventures of Huckleberry Finn* as "Mark Twain's enduring
  classic," for example—but don't make a point of bringing it
  up unless that reputation is key to your argument.

- **Go off-topic.** Keep your introduction streamlined and to
  the point. Don't feel the need to throw in all kinds of bells
  and whistles in order to impress your reader—just get to the
  point as quickly as you can, without skimping on any of the
  required steps.

6. Write the Body Paragraphs

Once you've written your introduction, you'll take the arguments
you developed in step 4 and turn them into your body paragraphs.
The organization of this middle section of your essay will largely be
determined by the argumentative strategy you use, but no matter
how you arrange your thoughts, your body paragraphs need to do
the following:

- **Begin with a strong topic sentence.** Topic sentences are like
  signs on a highway: they tell the reader where they are and
  where they're going. A good topic sentence not only alerts
  readers to what issue will be discussed in the following
  paragraph but also gives them a sense of what argument
  will be made *about* that issue. "Rumor and gossip play an
  important role in *The Crucible*" isn't a strong topic sentence
  because it doesn't tell us very much. "The community's
  constant gossiping creates an environment that allows false
  accusations to flourish" is a much stronger topic sentence—
  it not only tells us *what* the paragraph will discuss (gossip)
  but *how* the paragraph will discuss the topic (by showing
  how gossip creates a set of conditions that leads to the play's
  climactic action).

- **Fully and completely develop a single thought.** Don't skip
  around in your paragraph or try to stuff in too much
  material. Body paragraphs are like bricks: each individual

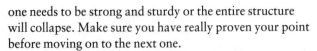

one needs to be strong and sturdy or the entire structure will collapse. Make sure you have really proven your point before moving on to the next one.

- **Use transitions effectively.** Good literary essay writers know that each paragraph must be clearly and strongly linked to the material around it. Think of each paragraph as a response to the one that precedes it. Use transition words and phrases such as *however, similarly, on the contrary, therefore,* and *furthermore* to indicate what kind of response you're making.

---

7. Write the Conclusion

Just as you used the introduction to ground your readers in the topic before providing your thesis, you'll use the conclusion to quickly summarize the specifics learned thus far and then hint at the broader implications of your topic. A good conclusion will:

- **Do more than simply restate the thesis.** If your thesis argued that *The Catcher in the Rye* can be read as a Christian allegory, don't simply end your essay by saying, "And that is why *The Catcher in the Rye* can be read as a Christian allegory." If you've constructed your arguments well, this kind of statement will just be redundant.

- **Synthesize the arguments, not summarize them.** Similarly, don't repeat the details of your body paragraphs in your conclusion. The reader has already read your essay, and chances are it's not so long that they've forgotten all your points by now.

- **Revisit the "So what?" question.** In your introduction, you made a case for why your topic and position are important. You should close your essay with the same sort of gesture. What do your readers know now that they didn't know before? How will that knowledge help them better appreciate or understand the work overall?

- **Move from the specific to the general.** Your essay has most likely treated a very specific element of the work—a single character, a small set of images, or a particular passage. In your conclusion, try to show how this narrow discussion has wider implications for the work overall. If your essay on *To Kill a Mockingbird* focused on the character of Boo Radley, for example, you might want to include a bit in your conclusion about how he fits into the novel's larger message about childhood, innocence, or family life.

- **Stay relevant.** Your conclusion should suggest new directions of thought, but it shouldn't be treated as an opportunity to pad your essay with all the extra, interesting ideas you came up with during your brainstorming sessions but couldn't fit into the essay proper. Don't attempt to stuff in unrelated queries or too many abstract thoughts.

- **Avoid making overblown closing statements.** A conclusion should open up your highly specific, focused discussion, but it should do so without drawing a sweeping lesson about life or human nature. Making such observations may be part of the point of reading, but it's almost always a mistake in essays, where these observations tend to sound overly dramatic or simply silly.

A+ Essay Checklist

Congratulations! If you've followed all the steps we've outlined above, you should have a solid literary essay to show for all your efforts. What if you've got your sights set on an A+? To write the kind of superlative essay that will be rewarded with a perfect grade, keep the following rubric in mind. These are the qualities that teachers expect to see in a truly A+ essay. How does yours stack up?

- ✓ Demonstrates a thorough understanding of the book
- ✓ Presents an original, compelling argument
- ✓ Thoughtfully analyzes the text's formal elements
- ✓ Uses appropriate and insightful examples
- ✓ Structures ideas in a logical and progressive order
- ✓ Demonstrates a mastery of sentence construction, transitions, grammar, spelling, and word choice

Suggested Essay Topics

1. *What role does Leper play in the novel? What does the author suggest about the nature of his relationship to Gene and Finny?*

2. *Discuss the importance of setting in specific scenes throughout the novel, especially in regard to what it reveals about characters and events. How do natural settings contrast with or complement the thematic content of certain scenes?*

3. *Contrast Brinker and Finny. How do their personalities relate to the winter session and summer session, respectively?*

4. *Discuss the symbolism of Finny's fall. Is A SEPARATE PEACE a novel of sin and redemption? Is Gene redeemed in the end?*

5. *Analyze the role of competition in the relationship between Gene and Finny. How does Finny's invented game of "blitzball" work as a symbol of Finny's approach to competition? Why is it significant that he excels at sports while Gene shines in academics?*

A+ STUDENT ESSAY

What makes Finny unique? How do those qualities affect his relationship with Gene?

In *A Separate Peace,* the adult Gene Forrester examines his final years at the Devon School, particularly his complex relationship with his best friend, Finny. The two boys are shown to have completely opposite perspectives on the world. Whereas Finny sees the world as essentially harmonious and benevolent, the distrustful Gene sees the world as rife with divisions. Finny's sense of completeness draws people to him, but the novel also suggests that he has an essentially childlike way of relating to the world, one that cannot survive the harsh realties of war.

The motifs of "wholeness" and "separateness" run throughout the novel, with Finny representing the former and Gene the latter. Finny seems to exist in perfect harmony with the world around him, a characteristic Gene notes again and again when he describes his friend's walk as a "flow." Finny's body seems to be a single, seamless entity, and his body in turn is at one with the whole world, buoyed along by its currents and free of tension from outside forces. This sense of harmony with the physical world extends to Finny's relationships with other people. Unlike the other boys, whom Gene describes as constantly constructing "Maginot Lines" against their real and imaged enemies, Finny never pits himself against others. Though he loves athletics, for example, he lacks the drive to distinguish himself. He refuses to let Gene tell the authorities that he has beaten the school swimming record, and then later invents a game, blitzball, where no one wins. Dividing people into categories such as "winners" and "losers" would defeat the true purpose of sports, in Finny's eyes: physically communing with the air and sky and engaging with a group of other players. For Finny, sports are an act of connecting, not of dividing. Tellingly, all the prizes he won at Devon were for sportsmanship, not for athletic prowess.

Gene, on the other hand, continuously divides the world into hostile and friendly camps. In his eyes, even high school sports games conceal fatal aggressions. Gene describes how he doesn't trust other athletes, vividly imagining football players "really bent on crushing the life out of each other," boxers caught in fights to the death, and tennis balls turning into bullets. Whereas Finny believes that "when you really love something, then it loves you back," Gene sees everyone as a potential enemy—even his best friend. Gene's mistrust arises from the fact that he not only believes that people can be divided against one another, but also that people can be divided against their very selves. He sees Devon as a place where everyone has "many public faces," appearing like scholars in the classroom, like "innocent extroverts" on the playing field, and like "criminals" in the smoking room. He's constantly struck by the sense that it is impossible to know what anyone might truly be like on the inside, and this anxiety leads him to believe that Finny harbors a secret hatred for him. Over the course of the novel, however, Gene comes to realize that his friend's public and private selves are fused into one whole—with Finny, what you see really is what you get.

While Gene remains wracked with guilt over his role in Finny's accident and eventual death, the novel seems to suggest that Finny could not have survived life after Devon. Gene knows that Finny's natural sense of empathy would be a liability on the battlefield; he teases him that he'd make a terrible soldier because he'd be forever confusing the lines between friend and enemy, inviting the Germans or Japanese to play baseball or accidentally trading uniforms with them. In a world sadly characterized by enmity and brutality, Finny's idealistic view of human nature seems a naïve notion better suited to schoolboys than to soldiers. Finny himself seems to understand this when, for all his insistence on unity and wholeness, he draws a stark division between his existence and the greater reality of the war. The "separate peace" of the title refers to Devon, the Eden-like enclave where young men can live as innocent children. However, while most of the students understand the division between Devon and the rest of the world to be a false one, constructed for their emotional benefit, Finny intently denies that the war even exists. He compartmentalizes his knowledge about outside events so that he can live fully and wholly in the moment, but as the boys grow up and begin enlisting, it becomes clear that Finny cannot keep perpetuating this lie and expect to survive the war.

As Gene notes, all the other boys of Devon experienced a moment when they found themselves "violently pitted against the world around them." Finny alone "escaped" this fate—the fate, that is, of growing up. Finny's death, though tragic, also manages to preserve his innocence, turning him into an eternal symbol of harmonious childhood.

GLOSSARY OF LITERARY TERMS

ANTAGONIST

The entity that acts to frustrate the goals of the *protagonist*. The antagonist is usually another *character* but may also be a non-human force.

ANTIHERO / ANTIHEROINE

A *protagonist* who is not admirable or who challenges notions of what should be considered admirable.

CHARACTER

A person, animal, or any other thing with a personality that appears in a *narrative*.

CLIMAX

The moment of greatest intensity in a text or the major turning point in the *plot*.

CONFLICT

The central struggle that moves the *plot* forward. The conflict can be the *protagonist*'s struggle against fate, nature, society, or another person.

FIRST-PERSON POINT OF VIEW

A literary style in which the *narrator* tells the story from his or her own *point of view* and refers to himself or herself as "I." The narrator may be an active participant in the story or just an observer.

HERO / HEROINE

The principal *character* in a literary work or *narrative*.

IMAGERY

Language that brings to mind sense-impressions, representing things that can be seen, smelled, heard, tasted, or touched.

MOTIF

A recurring idea, structure, contrast, or device that develops or informs the major *themes* of a work of literature.

NARRATIVE

A story.

NARRATOR

The person (sometimes a *character*) who tells a story; the *voice* assumed by the writer. The narrator and the author of the work of literature are not the same person.

PLOT

The arrangement of the events in a story, including the sequence in which they are told, the relative emphasis they are given, and the causal connections between events.

POINT OF VIEW

The *perspective* that a *narrative* takes toward the events it describes.

PROTAGONIST

The main *character* around whom the story revolves.

SETTING

The location of a *narrative* in time and space. Setting creates mood or atmosphere.

SUBPLOT

A secondary *plot* that is of less importance to the overall story but may serve as a point of contrast or comparison to the main plot.

SYMBOL

An object, *character,* figure, or color that is used to represent an abstract idea or concept. Unlike an *emblem,* a symbol may have different meanings in different contexts.

SYNTAX

The way the words in a piece of writing are put together to form lines, phrases, or clauses; the basic structure of a piece of writing.

THEME

A fundamental and universal idea explored in a literary work.

TONE

The author's attitude toward the subject or *characters* of a story or poem or toward the reader.

VOICE

An author's individual way of using language to reflect his or her own personality and attitudes. An author communicates voice through *tone, diction,* and *syntax.*

LITERARY ANALYSIS

A NOTE ON PLAGIARISM

Plagiarism—presenting someone else's work as your own—rears its ugly head in many forms. Many students know that copying text without citing it is unacceptable. But some don't realize that even if you're not quoting directly, but instead are paraphrasing or summarizing, *it is plagiarism* unless you cite the source.

Here are the most common forms of plagiarism:

- Using an author's phrases, sentences, or paragraphs without citing the source
- Paraphrasing an author's ideas without citing the source
- Passing off another student's work as your own

How do you steer clear of plagiarism? You should *always* acknowledge all words and ideas that aren't your own by using quotation marks around verbatim text or citations like footnotes and endnotes to note another writer's ideas. For more information on how to give credit when credit is due, ask your teacher for guidance or visit www.sparknotes.com.

Review & Resources

Quiz

1. During what year does Finny fall out of the tree?

   A. 1958
   B. 1942
   C. 1950
   D. 1939

2. What two places does Gene Forrester make a point of visiting when he returns to his school?

   A. A tree and a church
   B. A gymnasium and a classroom
   C. A tree and a flight of marble steps
   D. An athletic field and a classroom

3. What is the name of Gene's school?

   A. Exeter Academy
   B. The Devon School
   C. Deerfield Academy
   D. Lowood School

4. During the summer session, what do the boys do at the tree by the river?

   A. They build a tree house.
   B. They hunt for birds' nests.
   C. They chop off branches to make swords.
   D. They leap from a branch into the river.

5. What is the name of the club that Gene and Finny establish during the summer?

   A. The Super Suicide Society of the Summer Session
   B. The Blitzball Club of Devon
   C. The Young Marines
   D. The Air, Land, and Sea Society

6. What does Finny wear that causes such a stir at Mr. Patch-Withers's tea?

    A.   A bright pink shirt
    B.   A pair of polka-dotted suspenders
    C.   A Devon School tie, encircling his waist as a belt
    D.   A tie that is identical to the one that Mr. Patch-Withers is wearing

7. What is the name of the game that Finny invents?

    A.   Calvinball
    B.   Blitzball
    C.   Warball
    D.   Tree hockey

8. What kind of school record does Finny break in only one try?

    A.   A long jump record
    B.   A homerun record
    C.   A badminton record
    D.   A swimming record

9. How does Finny fall from the tree?

    A.   Gene's knees bend and he jounces the tree limb, knocking Finny off.
    B.   A branch breaks.
    C.   A gust of wind knocks him off.
    D.   He slips and falls.

10. What does Dr. Stanpole tell Gene about Finny's injury?

    A.   That Finny will be in a wheelchair for the rest of his life
    B.   That Finny's leg will heal so as to be stronger than before
    C.   That Finny will be able to walk again but that his days of playing sports are over
    D.   That Finny may die

11. Where does Gene tell Finny his own version of what happened on the tree?

    A.   At Leper's house
    B.   In Finny's home on the outskirts of Boston
    C.   In the boys' room at Devon
    D.   On a train

12. What job does Gene try to take to avoid playing actively on a sports team?

    A.   Football coach
    B.   Jump rope untangler
    C.   Chess teacher
    D.   Assistant crew manager

13. Who jokingly accuses Gene of having killed Finny?

    A.   Brinker Hadley
    B.   Dr. Stanpole
    C.   Gene's father
    D.   Chet Douglass

14. What does Brinker try to persuade Gene to do after a day spent shoveling snow off the railway tracks?

    A.   Join his secret society
    B.   Break off his friendship with Finny
    C.   Enlist in the military
    D.   Drop out of Devon

15. Why doesn't Gene join the army?

    A.   He is crippled.
    B.   He feels that Finny doesn't want him to.
    C.   He opposes the war.
    D.   He fears combat.

16. For what event does Finny claim to be training Gene?

    A.   The World Series
    B.   The Devon fencing tournament
    C.   The New England wrestling finals
    D.   The 1944 Olympics

REVIEW & RESOURCES

17. What is Finny's professed opinion of the war?

   A. That it will be over soon
   B. That it is a big conspiracy
   C. That it is morally wrong
   D. That Germany and Japan will win

18. Who becomes the first student at Devon to enlist?

   A. Finny
   B. Brinker
   C. Leper
   D. Gene

19. What kind of outdoor event does Finny organize?

   A. A winter carnival
   B. A tree-climbing contest
   C. A wintry game of blitzball
   D. A skating party

20. What happens to Leper in the military?

   A. He becomes a hero.
   B. He is placed in the navy and sent to the Pacific.
   C. He becomes a spy for the Germans.
   D. He has hallucinations and then deserts.

21. Who goes to visit Leper in Vermont?

   A. Finny
   B. Gene
   C. Mr. Prud'homme
   D. Brinker

22. Who organizes the "trial" to determine what caused Finny's fall from the tree?

   A. Finny
   B. Leper
   C. Brinker
   D. Dr. Stanpole

23. Who testifies that Gene knocked Finny off the tree?

    A. Leper
    B. Chet Douglass
    C. Brinker
    D. Dr. Stanpole

24. How does Finny break his leg the second time?

    A. He deliberately leaps from the tree.
    B. He falls through the ice on the Devon pond.
    C. He jumps out a fourth-floor window.
    D. He falls down a flight of marble steps.

25. How does Finny die?

    A. He kills himself.
    B. He is killed in the war.
    C. His broken leg becomes infected and he dies from a fever.
    D. A small amount of bone marrow enters his blood-stream and stops his heart.

SUGGESTIONS FOR FURTHER READING

BLOOM, HAROLD, ed. *John Knowles's* A SEPARATE PEACE. New York: Chelsea House, 2000.

BRYANT, HALLMAN BELL. A SEPARATE PEACE: *The War Within.* Boston: Twayne Publishers, 1990.

KARSON, JILL, ed. *Readings on* A SEPARATE PEACE. San Diego: Greenhaven Press, 1999.

SparkNotes Literature Guides

Visit sparknotes.com for many more!